what i did on my
midlife crisis vacation

WHAT I DID ON MY MIDLIFE CRISIS VACATION

Published by PiscAquarian Press

www.debbianne.com
Cover design by Lynda Mangoro, creative genius.

ISBN 978-0-615-52619-5

Set in Capitals and Cochin.
Paper sourcing certified by
the Forest Stewardship Council™ (FSC®) and
Sustainable Forestry Initiative® (SFI®).

to Patricia Lake

the coolest English teacher ever
who dished out perspective, encouragement, and
tough love in all the right proportions

I want to **acknowledge** and thank all the beautiful people who have helped out, particularly the heavy hitters—editors, advisors and personal cheerleaders—in this co-creation including, but not limited to:

Leo Chapeau, Daniel Reed Miller, Kimberly Skinner, Jenni Joy, Catherine Pelletier, April Delbrook, Michelle Smith, Lynn Swanson, Anthony Scarpelos, Cyrene Houdini; and the lovely and talented Lynda Mangoro especially for her patience, dedication, and vision.

I want to thank Joy Faulkner for her friendship, sunny demeanor, and linguistic brilliance, along with other creative souls whose delightfully quirky catch phrases I've adopted along the way. Beyond the overt contributions, many more have lent a hand, sometimes unbeknownst to themselves, because anyone who's ever crossed my path—from the rascally-est rabbit to the cutest fuzzy bunny—has taught me something, whether it's been through a multi-decade friendship or a stranger's meaningful glance rendered at precisely the right moment. They say we're all part of the same big jello mold—we merely *appear* as separate dishes of this gelatinous spirit-stuff. Big ups to all y'all.

Everything I've written here is honest and true from my perspective. Nearly all the names have been changed to protect the individuals' privacy (and in some cases, their good reputations), with the exception of certain high profile persons whose real full names appear intact.

I'd like to also **acknowledge** that the term woo or woo-woo or woowoo—which I'm quite fond of bandying about with faux disdain to point at all that is intangible, inexplicable, paranormal, supernatural, gestalt or just plain ridiculous—is probably derived from the Chinese word "wu" (as in *The Dancing Wu-Li Masters*) but I like to mix it up. If you're some kind of etymological purist (or any other kind for that matter), take heed: this will not be the last time I offend your sensibilities. It's only the first page, for chrissakes.

Enjoy! Your feedback is warmly welcomed at: www.debbianne.com

WHAT I DID ON MY MIDLIFE CRISIS VACATION

WHAT I DID ON MY MIDLIFE CRISIS VACATION

1

CUE THE CRISIS

"Confusion will be my epitaph."
♫ King Crimson

"Oh, it's just *way* too fucking much." Coming from a seasoned professional astrologer, the words were bittersweet relief. "I seriously do not know anyone who could handle this. Survive it, yes. But *handle* it? No way."

"Thank you...!" I managed to gurgle back. Finally, someone was dishing out some validation.

My astrology chart contained all the usual midlife crisis suspects, and heaped on top of those like some sick karmic sundae was an inordinate number of long, slow, drawn out, once-in-some-people's-lifetimes transits plus some intense pressurizing medium-range effects. The graphical ephemeris Bill created looked more like the polygraph of a fast-talking pathological liar. Neptune was engulfing me in a great twin-fog of confusion and delusion even as Uranus goaded me into making erratic changes. Chiron was busy re-opening my ancient wounds and pouring salt in them while Saturn had me ruthlessly scrutinizing things to the core. Not to be outdone, Pluto was steadfastly tending its alchemical mission, burning everything to the ground and leaving me to crawl from the wreckage. Though not necessarily in that order. There was nothing orderly about it.

And what exactly are these "transits," you ask? The short answer: a convenient analytical scapegoat for what ailed me. The real answer: the notable times when planets, wherever they currently are in the heavens, form significant angles to the locations those planets occupied at the time you came out of the womb. Some transits are quickies and others seem never-ending— it all depends on the relative speeds of the planets involved. Some are personal and others are sweepingly generational. How they get interpreted is a huge can of worms that I think I'll just keep the lid on, but suffice it to say that when a truly talented human astrologer is speaking, the stuff makes a whole lot of sense. My consultation with Bill Herbst arrived in divine timing to save my sanity.

I was feeling a lot of things, if not sane. My emotional terrain was largely sculpted in horizonless expanses of utter confusion, sprinkled with fleeting showers of clarity and saddled in periodic morasses of angst and depression. When depressed, I applied the tried-and-true home remedy of massive oreo-eating and movie-watching alone in the dark. So dark had been my outlook at times that suicidal thoughts came to call. I never seriously considered enactment though, fearing it would somehow screw things up for me in the afterlife, and I'd end up bawling "doh!" Homer Simpson style as it echoed down the canyon, ridiculing me for my foolish mistake. So instead I filled scrawly journals and notebooks with cheerful little observations and queries such as "what the hell am I doing here?" and "what is the point of all this anyway?" and "oh, god, please don't let me become a crazy old cat lady, celibate and living alone with nineteen feline housemates."

I had outward stability. I had community. I was in a pretty good financial position. I had the time and means to express myself creatively. I had the freedom to choose. But I also had the unusual burden of too much choice. Too much opportunity for discontent. Something was missing from my life, and it wasn't just a man—though that surely added to my discontent. But it wouldn't take a rocket surgeon to see how my mental state was not exactly a beacon for a healthy intimate relationship.

If anything, I was married to my house. I'd been busting my hump remodeling the joint, tearing into every square inch, rearranging nearly every molecule of it with my own bare (okay, gloved) hands. It was total immersion, and it provided a canvas for my art (big festive mosaic-tiled shower rooms, for instance) and for this reason I usually enjoyed the work thoroughly. But there was madness in it too: obsession and perfection-seeking, physical exhaustion and emotional breakdowns. I was starting to wonder if my health was being compromised by exposure to all the particles and fumes. For years, renovation had been the main recipient of my time and energy, having already reduced my formal work hours to sporadic part time, consulting, and part year jobs.

I'd been living in Portland, Oregon for an entire decade, and this was an astounding record for me. It felt more like a small town than a city because I couldn't go into a grocery store without running into people I knew—which made for a warm fuzzy existence for the most part. That is, until the very same conditions began to invoke social suffocation.

It was a decade of wild creativity. Moving to Puddletown immediately after my divorce, I got busy honing the fine art of *playing*. I took up music and singing. And dance classes. I dabbled in the bikey subculture. I started writing for the first time outside of academia. I held elaborate theme parties that became legendary within certain social circles, spending months envisioning, preparing, masterminding, decorating, and staging. People adored me for hosting these events, as they were crucibles in which they could loose their own creativity and assume character roles, socialize, meet new friends and lovers, and then rave about it all afterward. Those were high times in Portlandia.

But somewhere along the line, the fun-balloon was leaking its air. Not just because I occasionally had to huck some drunken rogue out on the curb or clean up horrendous after-party messes. No, something deeper was stirring. Waves of emptiness and discontent were beginning to wash over me with greater regularity.

My community was like family. Friends *are* my family, because my bio-family and I are from such radically different planets that I'd deemed it necessary to step out of their orbit long ago. But even chosen family can be dysfunctional (not to mention incestuous). After a while, I couldn't throw a small dinner party without someone's feathers getting ruffled because they hadn't been invited. I wondered if there could be such a thing as too many friends. We were growing apart—slowly. It seemed as if I was trying to figure out the meaning of life while they were contemplating what to wear at Burning Man. Little by little, I was withdrawing from the pack into my own cocoon, though I didn't rightly know it at the time.

Slightly soothed by the astrological assessment and newly equipped with the insight that this nuttiness was, to a large degree, my own custom crisis—and a finite one at that—I was able to relax a tiny bit. I could stop comparing myself to others and coming up puzzled when I asked them if they'd had or were currently having a midlife crisis of their own. Many people just sort of shrugged and responded with ambiguity. Trust me, if you've been in the throes of it, you *know* of it. Apparently not everyone has them; it's not some inescapable rite of passage. Which makes it all the more scoffable from the non-crisis-haver's perspective. People looking on may conclude that your life is just peachy keen and lacking cause for dissatisfaction, but this doesn't prevent you from feeling the way you do. If anything, it only makes you feel guilty on top of feeling crappy and confused.

What constitutes a crisis, really? Dictionaries will say things like "a crucial stage or turning point in the course of something," "an unstable period, especially one of extreme trouble or danger," or "a sudden change, for better or worse." As for me: unstable? Most definitely. Extreme danger? Not so much. Aside from my recent communing with power tools, I'd gotten most of the dangerous living out of my system as a teenager. But emotionally and socially dangerous, perhaps, yes.

It seems that most people, by the time they reach forty, find themselves saddled with kids, spouses, jobs, mortgages, relatives, and god-knows-what-else keeping their day to day life firmly anchored. Of course, many thoroughly enjoy the moorings and experience an uninterrupted lifetime of bliss in the harbor. Some even manage to set sail to new adventures with the whole brood in tow. Then there are others, like me, to whom a tether becomes a straightjacket, and who hunger to slash the ropes in the middle of the night, dashing boldly seaward, not knowing what serpents might rear their frightening heads but not really thinking about it either. Running away from home and joining the circus is not necessarily the answer, but that doesn't keep you from fantasizing about it.

The cliché midlife crisis goes something like this: Man meets Crisis. Man buys red convertible. Man takes to slippin' 'round with cute young thang. Man's wife feels victimized. Ugly divorce ensues. Lawyers laugh all the way to the bank. Crisis earns a bum rap.

Hence the term *middlescence*. Being an adult can be highly overrated. As for me, I had no dependents other than one beguilingly cute calico, so busting out of stasis was a relatively victimless crime—though you wouldn't necessarily know that if you were to query certain people in my life. I was beginning to consciously adopt the new manifesto of prioritizing self over others. And when you do that, believe me there's going to be some backlash from the ones who've been overwatering at the trough.

People often tell me I'm too young to have had a midlife crisis, but their assertions have more to do with their own feelings about aging (and a little to do with flattery). I've heard of people having them in their thirties nowadays. Crisis is in the mind of the experiencer. Who's to say where the middle of a lifetime falls, how long a middle transpires or a crisis endures? Well, when you find yourself basking in the sunshine of your life for the sixty-seventh day in a row and looking back at the dark hole you crawled out of, you can then know with some certainty that the crisis has been finite. And significant. But I'm getting way ahead of the story.

↯ ↯ ↯

Homeownership had been the cornerstone of my recent adult life. It made me feel secure—not just financially, but emotionally and socially. Upon joining the landed gentry, it was satisfying and empowering to think that never again could I be made to leave at the whim of a landlord, nor would I be restricted in what colors to paint the walls. Hell, I was tearing walls out and building new ones—total creative control. And yet, after nearly a decade the solidity of home-girl life was wearing thin. In fits and starts I wrestled with the futility of security in general and materialism in particular. I wanted to be free of it all, but paradoxically was still very attached to my creature comforts. It was tempting to jump on board with one of those "I only own 100 items" campaigns, but I don't think any of those people were in

6

charge of a geriatric wooden house. My tools alone would eat up the quota, let alone necessities like bubble bath and teacups.

Certain friends would say, "you already have less stuff than anyone I know," but that kind of comparison is useless. It's not a competition; it's personal. I was feeling burdened by what stuff I did own and started combing through it. It'd always been pretty easy to part with generic things that are easily reacquired, but now I was expanding the purging turf. Even my collection of memorabilia could no longer retain its sacred-cow status. I'd schlepped that heavy boxful in countless mooves, never once questioning its value or validity until now. It was mildly exciting to discover a frontier, to be able to cop a fresh look at old stuff. Why hold on to photos and cards from people I no longer knew or even cared about? Guilt might work for the Catholics, but it was an ineffective motivator pour moi. One by one, I held each item in my hands and considered how it felt when I touched it, looked at it, or thought about it. In each case, it quickly became obvious what to do: either keep it or chuck it. I think material things definitely hold energy and it can really bog you down if it's not an uplifting kind of energy. Call me a New Age bulimic, but I felt a hell of a lot better after purging.

Naturally, I was a big fan of the public library, because they took care of all the book owning, leaving me free to enjoy just the book reading part. It was win-win. And the Multnomah County Library system was probably among the best in the nation.

One day in my local branch, I was drawn to a certain hardcover by Sylvia Browne (an overly made-up scary television psychic). In it, she espoused a theory that our lives have five "exit points" written into the script. Interesting concept. Hmmm, if this was true, I was pretty sure I'd already passed on four of them, having survived a terrible car wreck, narrowly evaded bullets whizzing within a few inches of my cranium, experienced a near drowning, and emerged physically unscathed from another harrowing motor vehicle incident that left me pondering guardian angels and time-altering surrealism. If I really was careening toward my last exit, what then of the remaining miles?

Apathetic inertia was ever-so-gradually being transmuted into carpe diem, nothing-to-lose verve. If I was willing to die but didn't, I was then willing to live without the fear of death, or much else for that matter. I began, rather unconsciously and willy-nilly at first, to formulate a bucket list. It was all too easy to identify my dislikes and aversions, but... what was it that I really wanted?

2

ONE WAY TICKET
TO WOOLANDIA

"There's a world inside where dreamers
meet each other. Once you go
it's hard to come back…"
♫ Janelle Monae

For one thing, I wanted to see auras. Probably ever since I'd read *The Celestine Prophecy*—you know, that one chapter where the main character starts seeing energy fields around people as they interact, exposing all their ulterior motives and control dramas. As far as superpowers go, I found this one tremendously appealing, because I'd experienced a lot of bewilderment in my life from the chasm between people's words and my murky perception of what was *really* going on. I've often longed for that elusive telepathic society where "say what you mean and mean what you say" is simply a way of life.

My fascination with the paranormal, however, was kindled long before that James Redfield parable emerged on the scene. Mostly I blame the seventies for my strange obsessions.

⚡ ⚡ ⚡

The 1970s was a time of magic and innocence, other-worldly spectacle and paranormal possibilities, talking animals and cars, aliens, ghosts and witches intermingling with ordinary humans. Well, at least on TV it was. Like most American kids, I received a large part of my early education while plopped down in front of the tube (an actual tube, an old-school console television from yesteryear).

I loved watching reruns of *Bewitched, I Dream of Jeannie, Mr. Ed, The Flying Nun*, and *The Ghost and Mrs. Muir*. It seemed feasible that wiggling one's nose could produce any desired effect—I mean, shouldn't that be possible? I sure wanted it to be. *The Magic Garden* and *H.R. Pufnstuf*, whose creators were clearly experimenting with drugs, planted little seeds of altered reality into my impressionable young mind. And I found an exotic bounty of supra-human inspiration in *The Bionic Woman, The Incredible Hulk, Wonderwoman, Shazam!* and *Isis*. Really, it doesn't get much better than Isis—an ordinary chick transformed into an über-powerful goddess.

As the decade ambled on, new favorites emerged: *Mork and Mindy* (imbuing new meaning to the term miscegenation) and *The Dukes of Hazzard*. Can a car really jump across a canyon, land flat and keep driving? Sure it can. Evel Knievel did it on his motorcycle. Anything's possible, even a clean-cut lip-syncing family traveling around in a funky bus and getting paid to perform.* Those campy, goofy shows were a welcome contrast to the dysfunctional family reality show I was living in. I read some too, but TV watching was often the more peaceful activity at home once we stopped squabbling over what to watch, because there was tacit understanding that television was sacred. All conversations and sibling beatings automatically came to a halt when the commercials ended.

Of course I had a mood ring, a magic 8-ball and a Ouija board. I wasn't so naive to believe the ring was measuring moods, but I was more interested in the fun and wonder of the thing than in analyzing how it worked. I was simultaneously fascinated and frightened by Ouija boards because I'd been reading accounts of people becoming possessed by spirits with not-so-pure intentions. This was the sort of reading material I enjoyed at age nine—well, that and books about clairvoyance and ESP (extra sensory perception) and telekinesis and how time doesn't *really* exist in a linear fashion the way we think it does. (That time thing really blew my little mind, and the awe and puzzlement persist to this day.)

On rare occasions, I got to go to the old dilapidated movie house in our tiny town where they showed second-run, obscure, or otherwise cheaply acquired titles. (Sadly, it later became a triple-X establishment). Somehow I'd gotten wind of *Beyond and Back*, a grainy low-budget documentary about people who died, left their bodies and returned to tell about it—in other words, NDEs or near death experiences. I was completely gone—hook, line and sinker. I harangued my mother until she agreed to drop me off for a matinee with two bucks in my hand one Saturday while she ran around town, grocery-getting in her usual grand coupon-queen fashion.

Now, I understand that in the world of film, *Beyond and Back* is about as crappy and propagandistic as they come. But to my tender sensibilities it was utterly captivating, even as I was aware of its Christian bias. Each of the people "interviewed" in the film perceived an anthropomorphized image of God that was depicted in a re-

---

* That Partridge Family bus design later infiltrated more of my artwork than I'd care to admit.

enactment with (I'm sure) horribly rudimentary graphics. I wasn't fazed by the subpar quality—after all, this was the era when Atari video games were considered cutting edge. A philosophical floodgate in my mind had been sprung wide open. Thinking about stuff like that energized me, made me come alive, as if I was suddenly a full-color character in an otherwise black and white environment. I never once questioned the premise; it just seemed innately logical that we survive physical death somehow. I was (and am) neither frightened nor particularly affected by it. (Then again, I've never lost anyone close to me other than a few cats and my 97 year old great-grandmother.)

Aside from notable genetic longevity, my family was fairly typical of mainstream America. Not necessarily religious, we sometimes attended church simply because society seemed to demand it. We kids were occasionally subjected to Sunday school—and the greatest oxymoron known to child, Summer Vacation Bible School— but the motivation on the part of my parents was free babysitting rather than indoctrination. (I would later grow to wholly appreciate the areligious and apathetic nature of my upbringing. Much later.)

ϟ ϟ ϟ

I've heard of other people having existential epiphanies at age nine or ten, strange as it sounds. It was certainly a notable time for me, because after that my overt passion for the magical and mysterious went underground—presumably, sublimated in response to the changing pressures of adolescence. I stopped reading Tolkien and started playing Zeppelin. (Which, come to think of it, aren't all that disparate.) Cue the sex, drugs and rock-n-roll. Quick! before adult responsibilities creep in.

The year 1990 found me playing the part of a young corporate engineer. While sitting on an airplane one day (with a lot of leg room and empty seats, incidentally), I leafed through the airline magazine and found an article on Barbara Brennan. She ran an energy healing school in Miami, and what impressed me most was the fact that she'd been a NASA physicist before coming out of the woo-closet. She was a straddler of worlds, and holding that science card made her an automatic ally in my mind. I checked out her seminal book, *Hands of Light*, which provides the most detailed explanation of the human energy field that probably anyone has ever articulated, complete with hand-drawn depictions of what she sees clairvoyantly with her "high sense perception" skills. Clairvoyance literally means "clear seeing" which might imply that any optician's office would qualify as a clairvoyant training center. But since modern society, for the most part, has decided that auras are invisible or even imaginary, the "seeing" and the "see-ers" are largely relegated to the realm of weirdness at best, crackpotdom at worst. I was not immune to such cynicism, despite the fact that I believed wholeheartedly in invisible energy fields. I was a living breathing paradox. Brennan's book was interesting, but ended up back on the shelf to be ignored for many more years.

Then seemingly out of nowhere, in the early waxing days of midlife crisis central, she re-emerged in my thoughts, and I found myself online investigating her training programs. Maybe it was one of those Uranian flashes of inspiration (not quite like a hot flash, but we'll get to those later). By then I was looking for a new gig, something to sink my teeth into, so I formulated a bold plan: I would move to the east coast, someplace groovy like Athens, Georgia, and attend the Barbara Brennan School of Healing (BBSH) four year program. Not that one needed to live close by, because most of the students just flew in to Miami several times a year and otherwise worked at home, but I was ripe for an excuse to fly the coop. It seemed like a perfectly good circus to run away to, and a way to defer career decision-making for another four whole years. Perfect.

But going back to school was a huge commitment. And it's not the type of school that the government is just itching to hand you money to attend, so I had to be certain. The Brennan-ites don't permit you to drop in and investigate the school while it's in session (hmmm, should that have been a red flag?) so I settled for the next best thing. A couple of BBSH instructors were coming to Oregon and I registered for their weekend workshop, along with about a dozen strangers.

Well, if that workshop was any indication of the actual school's flavor, I'd be signing on for a mixture of heaven and hell. Sure, there was cool stuff going on, like subtle signs of energy healing at work, discussion of chakra vortices by people who can actually see and discern such things, and fascinating psychometry exercises. But when the kumbaya shit went down, I wanted to run for the hills. They literally had us holding hands, standing in a circle, and singing along to John Lennon's *Imagine* at the end of the program. It was truly gag-worthy. Oh, why must it always come to this?

Even so, I didn't want to make any hasty judgments (really, I'd already done so, but was in the habit of second-guessing myself) so I took another tack. I made private energy healing appointments with two local Brennan practitioners. During the sessions, I didn't really sense anything happening, so they seemed like mostly uneventful ninety dollar ventures. Well, except for a few little things, the value of which only became evident with a substantial passage of time.

The first practitioner was a young woman with purple hair who told me my energy was twisted up and that she had to sort of unfurl it. I would later come to directly perceive a similar kind of imbalance in my energy field and correct it myself, but at the time it just seemed like a whole lot of hooey—a claim that couldn't be substantiated, and a treatment that had no observable effect.

The other guy was not long on words, which made me feel even less satisfied with the expenditure, because if I don't feel anything directly I at least want to be told something interesting (whether I believe it or not is another story). What little he did say, however, was unsettling. He asked me if I'd always felt... uh... a little *different* and told me that when I realized "who I am" then a lot of things in my life would start to shift. Ponderous and useless sentiments. My mind jettisoned back to a boyfriend years ago who had drifted away, and the last thing he said was something about "finding out who I was." The supposition that I didn't know still really irked me. Although the Brennan healer never used the word "alien," that is precisely what he was hinting at. I'd never really doubted that life outside of earth was possible (and I loved those *Close Encounters* movies), but I definitely was thinking in terms of distinct "us" and "them" categories. I joked to my friends later on that, while there had certainly been suspicion in the past, there was now professional opinion lodged that I was a certified weirdo. Great.

Twice, I came very close to registering at BBSH. But given my less than stellar impression of her emissaries, it just wasn't going to happen. Besides, who was I kidding? I detested the humid climate of southern Florida, and a four year commitment was absurdly long for someone who currently changed her mind every few hours. So I did a little research and discovered some other options. It turned out there was a tiny energy healing school a few miles from home offering an 8-week course. Now *that* I could handle. I signed up and, along with four classmates, began my experiential foray into clairvoyance and energy healing. (It seems the two pursuits are inextricably linked. I reckon it's because you can't have power without responsibility. Dammit.)

My teacher, Janice, was extremely gifted in her ability to perceive energy and manipulate it—that is, she could actually clear away "stuck" blocks of energy. I know because I was flabbergasted after my first one-on-one session with her. She closed her eyes and waved her hands in the air while sitting across the room from me, narrating all the while about my old family emotional muck. An hour later, a vexing skin condition I'd had for years was suddenly completely gone. Results! Now that's what I'm talkin' about. The healing came as a pleasant surprise because I hadn't been focusing on the skin thing or even thinking about it at all.

Initially in class I was just going through the motions, trying to visualize energy running through my body in a twofold way as Janice described it: up from the earth through the soles of the feet, and down from the heavens or whatnot, through the top of the head, then mixing and taking a specific route through the chakras and the rest of the body. After three weeks, something amazing happened. I started to actually *feel* the energy in my hands. It was a big deal—something visceral to let me know, really know, that the energy was there and flowing. It was a gnostic confirmation, and a milestone at that.

We learned all sorts of fun visual tools for working with energy, a lot of them involving roses. For instance, if there were difficult relationships in our lives and we wanted to get some relief from energetic bondage, so to speak, we could imagine the other person positioned inside a rose and then destroy it. For some people, this technique seemed a bit too violent, but it was really just symbolic, and I loved it. The point was not to harm or disappear the person, but to get some breathing room and reclaim my own energy. Like most humans, there had been much interpersonal drama in my life, and apparently a lot of that emotional residue was still camped out in my aura. I found it highly amusing to be putting DeRoses into roses and blowing them up. I wonder if they felt the shift on some level.

We started practicing our newly acquired healing techniques on each other, and on friends and acquaintances or other willing guinea pigs outside of class. I was skittish at first, but slowly gained confidence in my tactile ability to sense energy. By practicing on live subjects, I got feedback and came to a fuller understanding of what I was perceiving with my hands. For example, I detected what seemed like a blockage in a woman's third chakra; it felt very different from the rest, as if a steel door was covering it. After our mini-session, I casually mentioned this to her and she started telling me all kinds of things that confirmed my reluctant "diagnosis." It was all very interesting, even if it was only marginally helpful to the other person. Most people seemed to appreciate and enjoy the attention, or at the very least found it relaxing. I had no particular goal other than indulging my curiosity. And helping people, if that was possible. Oh yeah, and seeing their auras. How could I forget that?

The actual seeing of energy was something that continued to elude me. But I was too enthralled with my newly acquired kinesthetic superpowers to care. I figured the visual part would come later.

⚡ ⚡ ⚡

On the heels of that breakthrough, it was becoming increasingly obvious that certain persons in my life were undermining me and acting as energetic vampires. I noticed with great clarity for the first time their manipulative and dishonest ways. Even more eye-opening was the recognition of a longstanding historical pattern in which I had played the role of easygoing sidekick to a series of domineering women in my life (doubtlessly, originating with my mother).

Janice helped me to understand what was going on energetically—well, more accurately, she shared her interpretation of the energetic patterns she saw. I was just feeling around in the dark of my own life, with my third eye as yet out-of-order, and I accepted her analysis of the situation without much scrutiny because it sounded pretty accurate. She really nailed some of the personalities of these people she'd never met, just by reading their energetic claws in my orb. There was no doubt that she was exceptionally gifted, but in retrospect, I realized her advice in handling my affairs was somewhat dubious because it was far more drama-infused and victim-oriented than was really necessary. Her ability to make the most of her gift was curtailed by her humanity, her personal filtration system. I learned an invaluable lesson: *being psychic does not necessarily equate to being wise.*

But ultimately, all is well, despite the awkward passages. I would have needed to issue some edicts and discontinue some of those unhealthy relationships sooner or later. Maybe Janice's counsel was just the brand of aura-storytelling needed at that time to induce in me enough indignation to spur important changes. I was learning to walk in my own truth, heading down the road to sovereignty, but I wasn't there yet. I was still getting periodically sideswiped into ditches.

⚡ ⚡ ⚡

I finished studying with Janice and was eager for more when a friend connected me to my next teacher: Lisa French, founder of the Clairvoyant Center of Hawai'i. The curriculum was similar, because both women had derived their teachings from the same original source (the Berkeley Psychic School), however circuitous the ride. Lisa was someone I instantly loved. She had all the psychic gifts Janice possessed and then some, with the added bonus of an ability to view human interactions with humor, compassion, and objectivity. I mean, this chick was *powerful*—but using her powers for good and not evil. Kind of like Glinda the Good Witch in the *Wizard of Oz*—she's the one you want in your corner.

Lisa and her protégés offered distance classes via conference call. I thought this was kind of weird and wondered how it could work, but went ahead and signed up anyway. Actually, it worked very well pedagogically, barring the occasional telephonic glitch, since the first few courses were given in Clairvoyant Meditation, and not hands-on healing. They did have energy healing classes in Hawai'i, but I would need to complete some prerequisites first. Since we were using our imaginations or our minds' eyes and since the energy knows no physical boundaries, it didn't matter where any of us were located geographically. The instructors were in South America and Europe, and one student was in China (now *that's* dedicated, with the time zone difference). If I'd had any doubts about my tele-instructors' abilities I couldn't hold onto them for long. They asked us to picture something, then made comments indicating that they could clearly see what I was visualizing. Kind of eerie. Well, some say telepathy is the way of the future, so I figured why not become an early adopter?

We continued the work of running energy through our bodies, and learned additional tools and tricks for healing and manifesting. I loved it because my mind was kept busy; I've always found it difficult to empty my mind of thoughts, and am easily bored by mantras after a while. With this type of meditation, the emphasis is on *fun*. As Lisa would say, "amusement is the highest vibration." Works for me, and the laughing buddha seems to concur.

It sure didn't hurt that I'd developed a tele-crush on one of my classmates. Even though we'd never met and I had no idea what he looked like or even how old he was, there was just something about Robert's voice and his laugh that was enticing. I looked forward to saturday mornings on the phone, sitting at home in my pink fuzzy robe and slippers with tea and kitty-love at the ready. And though it wasn't much, I at least had some semblance of committed routine in my life. That—and all the energetic grounding work I was doing for class—constituted an effective balm for my emotional maelstrom still percolating in the background.

↯ ↯ ↯

Comfy as life was in those fuzzy slippers, some invisible can-opener-wielding entity kept dropping by unannounced to open up can after can of discontent in my house. I started dreaming about Hawai'i. A lot. What could be more seductive to a disgruntled resident of a cold dark rainy city than thoughts of palm trees swaying, avocados falling carelessly from above, divine hot ponds, fresh coconuts, and dolphins leaping playfully just offshore of glorious sandy beaches?

Talk was cheap, and so were one-way airfares, so I formulated a new life-plan: I would continue my Clairvoyant Meditation class, but transfer to the in-person equivalent already in session on the Big Island. I'd stay there and keep taking classes until I became the clairvoyant superhero of my dreams. I rented my house in Oregon to some young chicks who were very happy to live there and even offered to take care of my cat. But I was reticent to take the leap, and I suppose I was sending out mixed signals to the universe because right before I split, the renters bailed suddenly. So I quickly switched to Plan B, a mini-version of Plan A. I would go to Hawai'i for a few weeks while friends assumed kitty-care housesitting shifts.

My arrival on the island was impeccably timed because Lisa French herself was teaching the class, and I hadn't met her in the flesh until then. She was hilarious! I just love a gal who can commune with spooks then turn around and crack up a room full of meatsuits without skipping a beat.

Another wonderful surprise was that my classmate Robert just happened to show up in Hawai'i and transfer to the same class that week. He looked nothing like I would have guessed, and was much younger than me. He had such a great smile and (I know this is going to sound so trite) *energy* about him. He was staying on an organic farm several miles away and hitchhiking around, so I offered him a ride after class. I was driving a borrowed truck that belonged to a friend of mine who lived part time on the island—the same friend who generously let me stay in his otherwise vacant sweet little cabin. It had a big beautiful walk-in shower complete with tile and volcanic rock mosaic art and a big window with a stunning view of the ocean. Ah, yeah, life was very very good.

19

Just as we pulled in the driveway at the farm, Robert decided to grab his things and come stay with me instead. I'd casually invited him to my friend's cabin, and apparently he needed no particular prodding or extended deliberation.

Well, I'm a bit too shy to get all Harlequin on your ass, but I will tell you that those few days we spent together seriously jump-started my mojo, which had been out of service for longer than was healthy. He was one of those spiritual-love-healer magical hippie boyz who wander the earth, loving up all the women in his path. But he does it so well that you'd never call him a player. He was sweet and fun, and yet masculine... how could I possibly not fall for him? I'll admit, I got greedy for just a minute, and made a weak attempt to apply that traditional girl-method of clinging, but really I knew it wasn't meant to be on ongoing relationship. He was a free spirit who had already hitched a ride on the next breeze. I simply had to appreciate it for what it was, and not be bummed for what it wasn't.

It just so happened that this romance showed up when the Uranus Opposition transit was exact in my astrology chart. Barbara Hand Clow wrote a whole book, entitled *The Liquid Light of Sex*, about this aspect of the midlife crisis, and after that magical fling I couldn't help but think the woman is on to something. A good hospitable Hawaiian lei was just what the doctor ordered.

⚡ ⚡ ⚡

I returned to my home-owning, cat-cohabitating, dreary-climate life, but it wasn't long before the wanderlust resurged. Surprise, surprise. This time I started thinking about France. I'd always wanted to go there, and the food, wine, architecture, language and political culture were beckoning more loudly all the time. I wondered if I'd ever become an ex-patriot, as things were looking pretty grim in the States at the time. Maybe I'd been listening to too much Portland pinko commie radio though.

I was pretty much broke at this point, having used all the cashish I had to fix up my casa. I'd done some odd jobs and temp jobs here and there, but with my erratic temperament of late, I wasn't really fit to hold down a "real" job. Anyway, I didn't have a clue what I wanted to do, and it wasn't that long ago I'd been feeling depressive death urges, so sitting at a desk all day seemed like a far more life-squandering experience than I was willing to endure. Everything I had was tied up in real estate equity and I wasn't emotionally ready to consider selling my house yet (did I even see that coming?), so I did what any good red-blooded American would do: go into debt. I wrangled a home equity loan through one of those Internet-fluff companies that were so abundant at the time, and freedom to roam was once again mine.

The trip to Europe commenced with a little eastward detour for some porcelain crowns. I was doing my part to bolster the world economy through dental tourism. In Budapest and Vienna I made three stellar friends through an online couchsurfing community. I'd selected them as hosts based on their general integrity, but to my surprise they were into meditation and energy healing, and turned me on to the Silva Method of Mind Control. (Sounds creepy, eh? It's not.) Oh, amazing universe that lines these things up!

I spent a month tooling around various regions of France, sampling pleasures of the palate while keeping always my woowoo soup simmering on the back burner. I had a lovely rendezvous with an American friend in Paris, then rode a bullet train to Bordeaux where a wonderful man showed me around town and cooked for me. Another young one. There was definitely sexual tension between us but I guess we were both equally reluctant to test the waters and risk crossing a boundary, thus becoming the rogue in a well-respected community network. Alas, I forfeited an opportunity for an exciting fling with a dashing young Frenchman. Actually, this would happen a few more times during the trip. What was wrong with me? I was so damn serious that I was shooting myself in the foot.

My next host took me salsa dancing and gave me the name of a preeminent energy healer in Nantes, the next stop on my itinerary. I traveled north and started feeling ill upon arrival, but staved it off with a lovely respite in Bretagne, thanks to yet another host—hostess, in this case. She was the only resident of her tiny hamlet in the couchsurfing database, and I had given up on her, having received no reply to the inquiry I made a month earlier. But it must have been fated, because suddenly she contacted me when I needed her most. And as fate would also have it, she was up to her eyeballs in spiritual woo-lore. Her husband was some kind of newfangled Buddhist motivational speaker who was friends with Eckhart Tolle and she urged me to read *The Power of Now*. I perused it, just as I'd done on several other occasions, but still couldn't find any substance to it, pronouncing it so much mumbo-jumbo as the *Time Magazine* reviewer had done, and replacing it on the shelf of their well-stocked library. *My* time, apparently, had not yet come.

I was drawn specifically to Carnac for les megalithes—a mysterious collection of carefully arranged honkin' huge rocks that purportedly had something to do with the winter solstice. I'm not sure what I expected to find there. It was hard to see the overarching patterns, but I walked amongst the rocks and pondered how the ancient people managed to move those heavy things around and why*. I found it even more puzzling that the locals didn't seem to have any answers, despite the fact that, presumably, humans have inhabited the region continuously since the construction. Whatever happened to the oral tradition? There tends to be an implicit assumption that society is ever evolving, and that we know more than our forebears did, but I'm not so sure about that. I suppose a good story was what I came for but left empty-eared. Maybe I was half-hoping for a mystical experience of some sort. But there would be none of that for me in France. Well, not unless fever-induced delirium qualifies…

A few more regions and many high speed trains later, during my final week in France the sickness caught up with me. It resurfaced in earnest with a sore throat on New Year's Eve, which was not helped by the fact that I stayed up all night. The new year greeted me with violent illness. I became so shaky that I could hardly stand up with my big backpack on. I found myself once again with no plans or reservations on a day when just about everything in the country was shut down. I say "again" because I'd foolishly gotten into the same

---

* I later learned that it was a sophisticated construction, optimized for its acoustical properties and likely used for sound healing of ancient peoples.

22

predicament a week earlier in Mont St-Michel. I decided to solve my problem then by splurging on the only available lodging—a very expensive hotel—and an eight-course Christmas dinner. It's amazing how efficiently the swipe of a credit card can wipe away stress.

New Year's Day I had a total meltdown in the Dijon train station. Using my lame high school French, I was trying to ask the agent—who responded curtly and disdainfully—how to get to the next town on my agenda. I thought I'd understood him, but ended up taking the wrong train. I came back, becoming very upset and feeling the final vestiges of strength leave my body. I nearly collapsed onto a bench with tears streaming down my face. Things that are quite simple when you feel good can become insurmountable obstacles when you're illin'. (I try to remember this always as I make my way through the world. How much unseemly behavior is readily explained by people's pain?)

A kindly man came over and asked if he could be of assistance. He was French, with a pretty good command of English because he'd spent some time living and working in the States. He patiently helped me to get the right ticket, to get on the right train that was also his train, to get off at the right stop and head in the direction of nearby lodging guaranteed to be open. As the train hurtled us along the iron rails he spoke calmly and softly—the way you talk to someone who's desperately trying to keep down some saltines and Seven-Up without hurling—distracting me from my misery with tales of his American firefighting adventures.

I managed to check myself in to a hotel and stay there for several days, in and out of sleep and fevered tremors. It was hellish and surreal. I hardly ate or even got up. I made one phone call—a very pathetic-sounding one, I'm sure—to a friend back home who does Reiki, asking her to send me some of that good long distance juju. The next day I was feeling a tiny bit better, not recovered by any stretch but able to stand up, check out and get myself to the airport. I had a lymph node the size of a tennis ball in the exact spot where my backpack strap had been rubbing, so I had to drag the thing behind me, looking rather hideously like Quasimodo-Tourist. It would be another whole month before I felt somewhat normal again, and it's rare that I even get sick at all, so this bout definitely gave me cause for reflection.

I thought about how my train station meltdown allowed that beautiful man to shine and give of himself the way he did, and perhaps in some small way redeem the image of his people from the old unflattering stereotype. (There's always a silver lining... even if I'm just clutching at straws). The broader message for me, I decided, was that I had been far too nonchalant with my energy field, so to speak. In those clairvoyant meditation classes, we learned how to protect ourselves from unwanted energy, and the tools work very well—if you use them. Which, of course, I hadn't. I thought back to a particular day in Paris when I was feeling exceptionally good, but ended up feeling super crappy a few hours later. When I persisted in drilling down into my memory I discovered an interaction with a surly person in which I apparently took on some heavy dark negative energy. It can happen... when you're unaware.

⚡ ⚡ ⚡

So I was becoming more cognizant of energy in its various forms and how it was affecting me personally, but there was still a clumsily large time lag involved in my revelations. I almost said I was becoming sensitized to energy but realized that I'd always been highly sensitive, and that was the very issue at stake. I was a natural born energy sponge—a clairsentient, or "sponge healer" as they say. It was my way of "fixing" things in my early family environment, but it didn't stop there (despite the fact that nothing ever really got fixed). Apparently I had been traipsing around trying to heal all of France with my belly: a valiant but foolhardy endeavor.

During my slow ascent back into the pink, every practitioner I went to see—be they energy healers, card readers, mediums, or especially tuned-in massage therapists—told me that the first thing she or he noticed was Mother Mary hangin' around. Well, the first time I heard that I must have rolled my eyes, because I was more than a little wary of name dropping, let alone brand-name-angel name dropping. But they say bringing comfort is her schtick, and if ever there was a time when I've needed it, she was right on the money. Sure, it's just a construct, an idea of a personality representing a bundle of energy, right? I don't really know, but I figured I shouldn't look an invisible gift horse in the mouth, so I just thanked the nice angel-lady and assumed it would've been even rougher without her. And if she does exist, I'm pretty sure that ex-firefighter in Dijon was under her employ.

3

MEDITATION BOOT CAMP

"I can't give up my good old
rough and rowdy ways."
♫ Jimmie Rodgers

The Vipassana ten day silent meditation retreat came highly recommended by a few people I know and respect, so I thought, "Why not? It's free, I'm unemployed, and I'm game for the adventure." I'd been practicing clairvoyant meditation on and off for a while and figured I should branch out and explore other styles of meditating. The dedicated quiet time free from everyday distractions was appealing, and if I didn't like their method I could just use mine instead. Who's to know? My mind is my own, the final frontier. And maybe, just maybe, I'd have some sort of mind-blowing experience. So there I was, actively participating in the demand side of India's spirituality export market. Shameful, I know, but it's true.

Arriving at the meditation center by bicycle, I attracted a lot of unwanted attention, so I found a bench away from the fray. On display was a circle of dudes talking shop in the human equivalent of dogs sniffing each others' butts. Inside, the registration process took place, albeit ever so slowly. They insisted that I fill out a form which I instantly recognized as the same form I had already completed online a month earlier. I'd made the mistake then of answering the questions truthfully, and this resulted in a game of phone tag and eventually a live conversation with a woman whose voice had the exact timbre of that invisible teacher in the Peanuts cartoons: *womp womp womp womp.* She turned out to be The Teacher at the retreat. This time I knew how to answer the questions to avoid scrutiny, though I doubt anyone actually read them afterward. What impressed me most during the intake process was that each person working there seemed to have all the joy and humor and much of the lifeforce sucked right out of them. Apparently it was very serious business, this enlightenment stuff.

Later, we womenfolk ate dinner and socialized, separated from the men until the end of the retreat. (They segregated everything, even down to "his" and "hers" jars of peanut butter.) I met a few really interesting women, one of whom had transplanted herself alone from Russia at the tender age of seventeen. Another was a Tri-met bus operator from Portland who swapped crazy #4 Fessenden route stories with me and commiserated about the wastefulness and corruption of her employer. By the time the second Seattle-ite asked me what it is that *I do*, I was rooting for the shut-up to commence—even before the conversation turned to extolling the merits of Burning Man. They confiscated our cell phones and car keys. (Are you thinking what I was thinking? As far as I know, no house deeds changed hands.)

The "noble silence" was lovely, but also trying. On the plus side, not only do you not have to make small talk with strangers, but it obligates you to ignore them. Unfortunately, that silence is filled with an endless cacophony of noises that humans are bound to create— clinking, slurping, coughing, sneezing, wheezing, breathing, snorting, gulping, yawning, throat clearing, snoring—all suddenly grotesquely amplified. It was strange to be crammed in like sardines with thirty people, living and eating side by side, without speaking or looking at each other. An interesting social experiment, really. They encourage your experience to be a head trip—by pretending to "work" in isolation —and this engenders some dysfunctional behavior, like people cutting in line or not yielding to others with no chance of verbal reconciliation. Walking through the hallways was like being inside a living Tetris game.

There was assigned seating for our group meditations and the woman stationed next to me was a really loud breather. Her exhalation was a cross between a gasp and a constipated sigh. After a few hours, evil thoughts starting coursing through my brain. It turned out she was hard of hearing, so unfortunately if I had strangled her, she wouldn't even have understood why. The one behind me fell asleep and broke into loud snoring every damn time, and I liked her for that, despite the snoring. But she had a bad case of old lady B.O. and that was kind of rough, olfactorily speaking.

These were the house rules (all but one of which I managed to break within 24 hours of arriving):

- No communication with each other or the outside world.
- No writing or reading anything (besides their propaganda).
- No food of your own.
- No sexual activity of any kind.
- No stealing.
- No killing.
- No telling of lies.
- No ingesting of intoxicants.

The daily schedule was somewhat grueling: wake up at 4:00 am, meditate for two hours, have breakfast followed by a short break, meditate another two hours, have lunch, then a slightly longer break, then four more hours of meditation, a "tea" break, three more hours of meditation and finally, lights out at 9:30 pm. The first morning, everyone slept in. I for one never heard the bell ringing at that godawful hour. The next day, The Manager came in and personally woke each violating sleeper with a flashlight and an insincerely zealous "Good Morning!!!"

During the long "group sits" in the Dhamma Hall (which I call the church), it was a real challenge to get comfortable sitting on the floor. My legs kept falling asleep. I tried every conceivable configuration of pillows and blankets and little benches, but it was only getting worse. I noticed that some of the older women had chairs reserved for them on the side of the room. I suppose I could've requested one, as they did, before the retreat began: me with the lifelong gift of poor circulation, me with the long limbs and resting blood pressure of ninety over sixty. But I hadn't, perhaps loathing to be classified amongst the old and infirm, or more likely because it just never occurred to me that I'd have no way of helping myself to a chair should I require one.

So I sought out The Manager, a horse-faced woman who I affectionately call Horsey—the same one who had sadistically woken me up earlier that morning. I assumed there was a simple solution to my problem, like "oh, the chairs are over there—go grab one." But instead she responded with weighty hesitance: "ummm… I'm guessing that The Teacher wants to talk to you. You should sign up for an interview tomorrow." Huh? *Interview?* What on earth did The Teacher want with me? Was it some grave offense to ask for a chair? Perhaps it's more pious to sit on the ground, and she was concerned that my enlightenment was at stake. Or was there some esoteric fable involving furniture that she needed to impart to a wayward heathen such as myself?

I signed up for the second slot out of ten interviews commencing at noon, then got myself to the church on time. But after interviewee number one came out, Horsey inexplicably, one by one, called in just about everyone else on the sign-up list in seemingly random order before addressing me. When she finally called me in, she neither acknowledged nor apologized for the illogical behavior and the fact that she had just wasted my limited break time. With managerial skills like that, this chick would be lucky to run the night shift in a Taco Bell. When I finally was able to converse directly with Ms. Womp Womp, she was actually quite reasonable and mercifully brief. And then... I had me a chair.

Naturally, I found the ordained schedule to be a bit obnoxious and started rearranging it to suit my needs. Sometimes we could "work" in our dorm rooms, and I seized those opportunities to nap. You couldn't really get out of the group sits because Horsey would stand in the back by the door like a bouncer until everyone filed in. If anyone was missing she left to round them up, and the proceedings came to a grinding halt until the stray cattle were herded into the church. When all was quiet you could hear the mooing sounds of actual cows on the adjacent property, which I found delightful.

Sometimes I snuck out to take a little hike. For our official short breaks, there was a small walking area provided as the only acceptable format and locale for exercise; even yoga was disallowed, as it might cause "a visual distraction." That sanctioned area was so small and crowded, it was like a Habitrail for humans, and only slightly more roomy than the halls inside the building. I sorely needed some real exercise to get my blood circulating again and I discovered a really nice trail in the woods, just beyond those pesky signs forbidding students to venture outside the Habitrail. The retreat's locale in the Cascade foothills was gorgeous: snow-sprinkled mountains off in the distance, a charming meadow in the foreground, and a patch of fir trees in between, all teeming with frog life by night, bird life by day, and prancing deer and bunnies if one was lucky enough. Ah, nature—now that's good meditative fodder.

The church housed a collection of floor mats and had an invisible wall down the middle: boys on the left side of the room, girls on the right. Up front was a high platform where The Teachers sat, one of each gender, facing their appropriate halves of the constituency. Behind them were two huge wall-mounted video screens. This created the doubly invasive experience of not one but two larger-than-life projections of the cult leader... err, excuse me, guru—a certain Mister S.N. Goenka. The footage was from 1991 and he looked pretty darn old then, so I wondered if he was still alive or whether we were taking orders from some raving dead lunatic. Would they even let on? Maybe they'd carry on as if nothing happened, the way the Rolling Stones continue to prop up Charlie Watts at the drum kit. The program was so regimented that I couldn't imagine them being able to adapt or modify it.

The Teachers entered the church via mysterious chambers behind the stage, as did their select group of devotees who sat close by —those exalted volunteers who made our food and kept the place running, and who had, themselves, taken the course many times before. The Teachers sat in lotus position, motionless and without expression, draped in white blankets atop big white cushions. Ms. Womp Womp looked a lot like the secretary in my high school principal's office who was known to the student populace as "Old Stoneface." When I first saw her close up during the chair negotiation, I was shocked to realize she was probably only about forty years old. The male Teacher did all the talking. Which wasn't much, because his job consisted mainly of pushing buttons on the A/V equipment. (I suppose that makes him a professional button pusher.) He was a youngish gay guy with an unfortunate haircut, who was clearly taking his role *very* seriously. The positioning of the two Teachers on stage mirrored the projected images of Goenka on screen, always with his wife stationed silently to his left. I found the dowdy gender rules highly ironic considering the high percentage of gay people involved in the operation.

Meditation sessions usually began with audio recordings of Goenka chanting, followed by a series of stern authoritative in-your-face commands repeated ad nauseum. Now, here was a man who loved the sound of his own voice. He was fond of repeating his last phrase two or three times and pausing for dramatic effect between

32

refrains, and did this continually. The chanting sounded so ludicrous, I was amazed that no one else seemed to notice. Imagine what sounds like an extremely inebriated man with a thick Indian accent, rottenly and incomprehensively half-singing some long forgotten tune, and at the end of each line, trailing off into a gravelly, decidedly unmelodic low pitch using up all the air in his lungs. Then there's a brief silence in which you fully expect to hear a loud hiccup or belch. It kind of reminded me of Grandpa Simpson launching into a wicked bout of snoring, mid-story.

How I longed for a good set of earplugs! After a while, though, I started getting used to it and seeing the entertainment value. I inadvertently laughed out loud once—thankfully no one noticed or acknowledged it if they did. On Day Four, Goenka's vocal stylings turned funky, almost rap-like.

Years ago, I attended a Buddhist ceremony in which everyone was chanting together with the beads and the hey-nenny-nenny an' all. They passed around books with phonetic versions of the words so you could chant along; after all, the idea was to drown out the monkey brain chatter with repetitive sounds. This Vipassana thing wasn't like that at all. The chanting was Goenka's wacky performance art that you simply had to endure as part of the indentureship. It was impossible to follow along because there were no visual aids, and the man seemed completely incoherent (unless you happen to speak Padi, and even then…). Besides, you weren't even *supposed* to participate, except for the very end when everyone would repeat a certain phrase after him three times while bowing down. That was super creepy to witness people saying something in unison that they don't understand while lowering themselves before a video-projected guru. It was definitely the beginning of the end for me.

One day I was strolling on that illicit lovely wooded trail when I saw another woman heading my way. My first thought was "yeah! another renegade—we're gonna become fast friends…" but as we neared one another she flashed me a weak phony smile and radiated an unmistakable hate-vibe in my direction. It dawned on me that she was one of the devoted ones in the front row at church. Oh, well, at least I'd know who the narc was if I got busted. Which is exactly what ran through my mind the next morning when Horsey came to inform me that The Teacher wanted to see me at 7:25 am.

But no, that wasn't it. Ms. Womp Womp wanted to give me a make-up session for the 15 minutes of group sit I'd missed the previous evening. The sessions had been running painfully long and late, and after two and a half hours of being talked at by The Most Annoying Man in the World, I just couldn't force myself to go back in there after the break. I think I really hit my wall when he started yammering about the dining hall. He was doing one of his not-so-funny comic routines, and this one was about the part where no dinner is served and how people will try to eat an extra plate of food for lunch to compensate but they ought not to. Feeling hungry and hypoglycemic while having an overweight, overly sedentary and unhealthy looking man tell me, possibly posthumously, that I ought to be eating less food was about all I could take.* I had already signed up for the last shower of the night, so I decided to get on with the getting clean business. Horsey was all up under my grill before the water hit the shower floor. I told her flatly that, no, I would not be returning to the hall that evening.

Ms. Womp Womp was deeply and sincerely concerned that I had missed out on some critical Goenka-speak. She started regurgitating his words to me, but it was nothing new. I had, in fact, already heard this part of the spiel—very exciting stuff having to do with concentrating on your nostrils—but apparently one cannot possibly understand a thing until it's been repeated thirty-seven times. It was getting to the point where hearing that man utter the word "knowstrils" was triggering psychopathic urges in me. How's that for engendering peace and love, Mr. Goenka?

The next time I ventured out for a hike, I encountered the same narc-chick, plus two men who were also servers, presumably. Each one looked at me with such squinch-eyed deep reproach that it was almost laughable. If these were the purified minds, I'd just keep

---

* They never did explain the reason for not having dinner. It wasn't for health, since full-on fasting was prohibited. Maybe it just keeps their budget down. But probably they believe suffering is good for you.

mine defiled, thanks. I'm not sure what bothered them more: the mere act of defying the rules, or the idea that I was wrongfully sharing in *their* entitlement—one of those little bones they'd been thrown to help entice them into giving more of their time and energy, and possibly money, to the cause.

Back on the compound, my friend the narc marched right into Horsey's office, then came out and looked me directly in the eye (a rare occurrence at this silent retreat). She did not literally stick out her tongue but she might as well have. Then the bell rang for church— earlier than usual. Either my clandestine timepiece was broken or they were calling a special meeting, probably to publicly shame me for my outlaw behavior. En route to the church, Horsey pulled me aside and reprimanded me to stay on the Habitrail course. "No problem," I told her honestly, since I was already milling over the idea of an early departure. The whole thing was like being in girls' boarding school, but it just wasn't that hilarious without Tootie and Blair around.

It turned out we were starting early because Goenka had some additional ranting to do that day. It was the transition from the intensely-monitor-your-nose-hairs days to slightly more exciting times. We would be employing a technique called Anapana that entails being singly focused on one's breathing. I've never known anything to be quite so oppressively boring. I know it's worked wonders for some people, but to me Vipassana just seemed like a vestigial Goliath of a tool. Surely there are many roads to Enlightenmentville, but this was like going by Conestoga Wagon over muddy rutted roads when Lear Jets are available.

⚡ ⚡ ⚡

"It's a good day to ride," I thought to myself. With clear blue skies and seventy degree air in early May, I couldn't resist a jailbreak-by-bicycle shenanigan. Sure, I could've just gone and told them that I'd had enough and would be leaving, but where's the fun in that? No, I wanted to plot a getaway. I knew exactly when and how I would do it. And petty as it sounds, I wanted it to be a minor disruption to the order of the day. I wanted Horsey to feel just a little bit less in control, if only for a moment.

Unlike the other participants, I hadn't handed anything over to the authorities at the onset, and I'd stashed my bike in an unlocked building nearby. That morning, I packed everything up after breakfast and waited for Horsey to come out ringing the gong for the first group sit. As she headed down the path to the church, I grabbed my bags and bolted in the other direction. Before long I was out riding in the sunshine, wind in my hair, all the appropriate theme songs playing in my head. I pretended I was under duress, that they'd be coming after me, and this made the escapade all the more silly and fun. I was having such a great time that I thought, "Ahh... so this is what they mean when they say you'll leave here feeling blissed out."

And just for extra self-amusement, I had left a note behind that read: "So long... and thanks for all the fish!"*

---

* No, they weren't feeding us any fish. It's a Douglas Adams thing. I silently gave thanks for the food they provided every day. It was tasty and healthy, if lacking in protein and frequency, through no fault of the servers.

4

HALLELUJAH!
PUT YO' HANDS ON THE... CRYSTAL?

"Surprise! You're dead.
Guess what? It never ends..."
♫ Mike Patton

I was really looking forward to visiting an obscure little town in northern Florida that I'd heard about for years—oddly enough, from my own mother who wanted very much to go but somehow never managed to do it in all her years of Florida residency. All I knew about Cassadaga was that a lot of psychics lived there. And that was enough.

I was on one of my madcap multi-modal travel adventures, and I hitchhiked a ride from the nearest train station. The guy who drove me was a wee bit "off"—probably taking more than his share of meds —but harmless enough. We stopped at a yard sale en route, and I found this amusing, wondering if the other people there assumed we were old friends or even a couple. How wrong they would be.

Ten miles later in the dusty afternoon heat, we arrived in the one-horse psychic town. I was genuinely surprised at how much of a tourist trap it was. I'm not sure what I was expecting… perhaps a self-contained universe in which I was going to have to knock on people's doors and coax them into letting me join their secret society. Well, I'm nothing if not self-entertaining.

There were signs posted everywhere advertising the services of "certified mediums" (who certifies them, anyway?) and offering 31 flavors of psychic readings. Whether you wanted to converse with dead folks, angels, spirit guides, animal totems, or probably any other sort of beings, you could do it here. There were the requisite gift shops brimming with crystals, beads, incense and other New Age staples, and an impressive bookstore with entire shelves dedicated to the Tarot, UFOs, and past-life regressions, among other fascinating subjects. But the commercialism and hawkishness needn't cast unwarranted doubt on the legitimacy of the mediums. After all, bills need to be paid. And this "theme" town had been in effect long before the term "new age" entered the vernacular; it was a Spiritualist Camp established in the horse-and-buggy days of 1894.

I stayed at the old Cassadaga Hotel, which was in fact the only hotel. It had a certain charm to it and the staff proudly announced that the place was haunted. I'm guessing that was a big draw for certain X-Files-watching tourists. In the morning, a fellow guest asked me eagerly, "Well?! Any apparition activity?" Nada. The clerk raised an eyebrow in surprise. Apparently the previous occupant of my room had to be relocated. "It was too crazy in there for him. They must like you," she posited. Huh. Or maybe I just have good spirit bodyguards.

Inside the hotel was a little restaurant called the Lost in Time Café. It was truly lost to me, as I never did get to eat there due to the very un-businesslike manner in which it was run. Posted hours were limited to weekends, 11 to 5, and when I showed up at 4:00 on Saturday I was told rather unapologetically that they decided to close at 3:00. Well, this *was* the South, so I suppose I just needed to chill out and adjust my attitude, just as they had so effortlessly adjusted their schedule.

I was pretty hungry and carless and the nearest town selling foodstuffs was a good sprawly non-pedestrian-friendly humid Florida mile away. (Beware of locals bearing directions; a Florida mile is not equivalent to an actual mile—it is much longer.) My bohemian travel adventures do have their little foibles from time to time. For the duration of my stay I subsisted on snacks I'd brought with me, and mercifully, a home-cooked meal courtesy of my new friend Margot.

I met Margot while sitting on the bench outside the bookstore. We struck up a conversation, initially about astrology but morphing into her favorite subject—the Kabbalah. She was something of an odd bird, which endeared her to me, and she'd somehow, in her near-retirement years, found her way to this unique community of which she seemed a tenuous adjunct member at most. In gaining her trust, I became privy to some very interesting snippets from her life. Like the time she was babysitting and saw the likeness of a full-grown man hovering above the fussy baby, exclaiming in exasperation, "I'm from Alpha Centauri and I'm having trouble staying in the body!"

Margot brought me along to a full moon party, which turned out to be a comical scene. I wondered if this would be the last time I witnessed the spectacle of a Native American wannabe white guy banging on hand drums, passing around a pipe, chanting outrageously, and at the end soliciting cash for services rendered. For a minute I completely forgot I was in Florida; it could have easily been the Pacific Northwest. Or anywhere really. United we stand in ludicrosity. (For all I know, the dude was Sitting Bull in his last lifetime... and an actor this time around).

39

As far as towns go, Cassadaga was pretty darn cute. The original settlers had mostly come from Lilydale, an older Spiritualist community in upstate New York, and they brought with them some Victorian architecture—a rare treat to behold in Florida. The town was pleasingly compact, so I could pretty much walk everywhere, including the church. Stationed there over the weekend, I seized the opportunity to attend the Sunday Service. I really had no idea what Spiritualism was about, but I was up for the adventure. If nothing else, I knew I'd enjoy the quaintness of small town churchgoing (especially if the ladies wore fancy hats), safe from the pressures of conversion because I would be leaving town the next day.

Unlike every other church I'd stepped foot in, there was no sign of Jesus in there. No cross, no saints, no evidence of any ties to Christianity, and yet, it had that distinct churchy feeling—both strange and familiar. The congregation was an eclectic mix, or more precisely, a mix of eclectics. The average person was middle-aged, female, open-minded and -hearted, with a fiercely independent sense of fashion. A pack of teenagers, or possibly young twenty somethings, tumbled in after the service began. I eyed them curiously, wondering what their story might be, because the only other young'ns present had clearly been dragged along by their parents. I interviewed the posse afterward and learned they'd driven two hours from the university in Gainesville to witness firsthand the exciting events they'd been hearing about for many months.

A heart-shaped wreath hung high on the back wall of the stage where a rather hip band was playing. The musical line-up consisted of a guitarist, a keyboardist, a lady-reverend singer and a gentleman percussionist who was clad in elaborate African garb. All of them white baby boomers. Initially, the tunes were innocuous enough: *Will the Circle Be Unbroken* and *I'll Fly Away*, or even *Amazing Grace* (though possibly the honkiest rendition to ever fall upon human ears). The hymnals contained some Christian standards too (how did I even know that? From those handful of times hangin' with the Presbyterians long ago?) along with Spiritualist smash hits such as: *Voices Talk to Me*, *Come Thou All Transforming Spirit*, and *Flow, Spirit, Flow* or the ever popular *Shall We Know Each Other There?* In between hymns—which

40

incidentally, you have to stand up for and pretend to sing along, just like in regular church—there would be a little speech given. But not about damnation and hellfire. It was about the importance of positive thinking! What a splendid surprise.

Then the real show began. The special guests were a pair of identical twin brothers from England—both mediums, both preachers. The men were about sixty, each with a shock of thick grey hair almost in the shape of a pompadour. They wore matching eyeglasses, and suits and ties (not matching in color, thankfully). Both were dead ringers for a flesh-and-blood version of Dilbert, the iconic cubicle-dwelling comic strip character. One of the brothers had a kind of Liberace flair and boisterousness to him. They took turns relaying messages to members of the audience from those members' dead relatives. "May I speak to the lady in the third row wearing pink, please?" Presumably it's the loudest or brightest, most insistent spirit who gets heard above the din. The Dilberts took care to first describe in great detail the spirit's formerly incarnated personality, so as to remove all doubt. The message recipients seemed pleased and honored to be chosen and did generally acknowledge (if only subtly) the accuracy and relevance of what they were hearing.

This, I learned, was the primary tenet of Spiritualism: to "prove survival"—to demonstrate the fact that we are spiritual beings who transcend the demise of our human bodies. Which is a pretty helpful authentication, if you stop and think about how much trouble has been caused in the world by the fear of death.

The Dilberts were talking at hypnotic hyper-speed, almost like auctioneers. ("*We've got one dead grandma here, two dead grandmas... do I hear three?*") The flamboyant one would intersperse his narratives with "do you understand me, dahling?" The stunned recipient usually nodded slowly, deer-in-the-headlights style.

I found this "message service" pretty exciting because I'd recently been engrossed in Arthur Ford's autobiography, *Nothing So Strange*. Ford was a famous traveling trance medium during the 1920s

41

through the '50s.*   He routinely sold out large venues with his mediumship act and occupied newspaper headlines at times, including a famous publicity stunt involving magician Houdini and his wife. It would have been so cool if the Dilberts were trance mediums, but apparently it's just not done that way anymore. I guess every field has its innovation, and mediumship is no different. With the old trance method, a spirit would take over the medium's body completely. The "host" went unconscious and was fairly drained afterward with no recollection of what had taken place. So it seems like the newer method is more akin to channeling (at least certain varieties of it, from what I understand), because the messages come through while the host remains conscious and in control. Better for them, but less flashy for us.

Next came the hands-on healing. There was no big rapturous scene in which a crippled man suddenly throws down his crutches and walks. (Damn.) It was more like a room full of people doing Reiki. Very mellow. Chairs lining the back wall that remained empty until now were suddenly filled with bodies eager to receive the energy— myself included—while the healers stood behind the chairs and lovingly laid their hands on heads and shoulders. Meanwhile the presiding preacher-guy narrated a guided meditation. Enhanced by some tasteful live percussion in the background, it was a good one— the kind that transports you elsewhere, at least for a few minutes—and the place effused a truly angelic, lovey-dovey vibe. I almost forgot I was in church until the collection plate came around.

After the service, we all walked up the hill in the Florida sunshine to another building where lunch was served (hooray! said my stomach). Another full hour of message service transpired—this time

---

* I learned about Arthur Ford while reading *Walking Through Walls* by Philip Smith. It's the dad version of a momoir, and the author's eccentric father, Lew Smith, who was a cohort to Arthur Ford in the 1950s. After Ford's death, he continued to talk to Smith from the other side, commanding his incarnate pal's attention by causing the lights to go on and off in a particular sequence, wherever Smith happened to be located at the time. This included public places such as restaurants, to the chagrin of Smith's then-teenaged son (the author) who wanted nothing more than to be "normal." Funny stuff.

with a whole cadre of mediums, some of them students in training. I found this rather intriguing, the idea that one could be *trained* in mediumship.*

I became a bit restless and bored with the service. Maybe because none of the messages were for me. They started to sound all the same... at least until the student mediums delivered them with slightly more pizazz and less decorum. A typical message came to a middle-aged woman from her mother or grandmother, expressing love and support, and also specific advice or insight into some current family drama. Probably if they had called on me, the message would have bored other people to tears just the same.

The next day, Margot kindly drove me to the train station, but not before I wrangled a personal reading from one of the local practitioners-for-hire. Among other things, she told me about a relationship I was going to have with a man a couple of years my senior whom I already knew. I wondered if I had chosen the only untalented psychic in town, because after quickly scanning the ranks of friends and acquaintances in my mind for a possible boyfriend, I came up blank. It would be another year before I'd have the "aha!" moment about her predictions.

⚡ ⚡ ⚡

Two years later, I had completely forgotten about Cassadaga when I was walking around San Francisco with a friend. We found ourselves standing on the sidewalk staring right up at a Spiritualist Church. It was on the same street as the Christian Scientists and Unitarians—apparently we'd wandered haphazardly into the city's fringe religion district. I was thrilled at the discovery, and marked my calendar to attend services the following Sunday.

This one had a markedly different feel to it—about as different as San Francisco is from small-town northern Florida. The church itself was an architectural marvel built in the 1920s of grand old trees,

---

* For a while I strongly considered attending the famous Arthur Findlay College in England, where Spiritualism apparently first sprouted. It was just one of the many wacky lifeplans-that-wasn't.

43

plate glass and tile. And naturally, the folks attending were diverse as all get-out.

The service began with energy healing in the ornate back room of the church, where anyone desirous of healing vibes was welcome to step in and get some. There, a beautiful chipper Chinese-American woman played old jazz standards on the organ, her feet barely reaching the pedals. She seemed to be both six and sixty at the same time.

"Spiritual healing is an act of divine love," said the head reverend, a brilliant and gentle octogenarian. He was one of five healers working that morning. A large rotund man of few words stood at the entryway like a benevolent bouncer, mentally keeping track of all who entered, then calling on them in perfect order despite the willy-nilly seating—a daunting task handled with impressive skill. (This reminded me of how orderliness is one of the most pleasing by-products of British culture. Some contrasting experiences in France had given me newfound appreciation.)

The main church service began. After sending our collective healing thoughts to a list of absentee persons-in-need, we all stood for a hymn—a corny one entitled *He Leadeth Me: O Blessed Thought*. Then, together, we read aloud the Declaration of Principles:

1. We believe in infinite intelligence.
2. We believe that the phenomena of nature, both physical and spiritual, are the expression of infinite intelligence.
3. We affirm that a correct understanding of such expression, and living in accordance therewith, constitute true religion.
4. We affirm that the existence and personal identity of the individual continue after the change called death.
5. We affirm that communication with the so-called dead is a fact, scientifically proven by the phenomena of Spiritualism.
6. We believe that the highest morality is contained in the Golden Rule, "Do unto others as you would have them do unto you."
7. We affirm the moral responsibility of individuals, and that we make our own happiness or unhappiness as we obey or disobey Nature's physical and spiritual laws.

44

8. We affirm that the doorway to reformation is never closed against any soul here or hereafter.
9. We affirm that the Precepts of Prophecy and Healing are divine attributes proven through Mediumship.

I thought number four was particularly interesting, because for some reason I'd been under the impression that the individual personality goes away with the physical body, and what's left of us gets folded back into the giant vat of soul-cookie-batter, to be doled out in new succinct blobs onto various baking-sheet lifetimes (and hopefully not burnt to a crisp).

Normally group recitations give me the creeps, but I was okay with the Spiritualists. Most of what they're saying is amenable to my worldview (although I'm not sure I understand the "reformation" part of number eight...) It's definitely old school; their spiel hasn't really changed in 150 years. It's not hard to see how they were likely considered heretics back then—struggling against powerful established churchianity—and needed to band together for support. After all, that's the whole purpose of church, is it not—strength in numbers and bonding via shared belief systems? Nowadays, their righteous mission seems about as necessary as humans having tails, but it's fun and interesting to attend their shindigs nonetheless.

I ended up going back several times, and caught some inspiring (and sometimes even slightly humorous) talks on sacred geometry, spirit guides, psychometry, mediumship, and notions of "following a spiritual path as a human being." I loved these "sermons" because the reverends—of whom there were several—were mostly over eighty, and it just tickled me so to see and hear them speak of chakras and energy and the law of attraction. They were the grandpas and grandmas of my dreams! It's amazing how a certain phrase uttered by a smug New Ager can be irritating, yet when a jolly old codger speaks those same exact words, it's suddenly delightful.

I loved the musicians and the music—well, the secular selections at least—and the musical zeal of the head reverend. After giving a short talk he'd say things like "let's have some rhythm and harmony" or "now let's have some lovely music to set the vibration." The main organist, who was also a harpist, was then stationed at the grand piano near the altar, and she played beautifully, expertly, happily. Sometimes the reverend would sing one of his favorite hymns as a solo, but either way he was standing up there emanating pure joy, looking childlike at the podium, eyes closed in ecstatic reverie. Soon after, they collected the "love offering" to help pay the bills. It was about as low-key a plea for donations as I'd ever seen, and their humility made me want to open my wallet even wider.

In fact their approach, on the whole, was extremely laid back. No proselytizing whatsoever. Heck, their printed materials were so obscure and poorly written that dissemination outside of those in-the-know wasn't even a faint possibility. The congregation was hardly robust—downright diminutive compared to the glory days of Spiritualism past. But there was a steady, if small, influx of new visitors who found their way to this odd place, fueled always by curiosity about the message service.

The reverends shared mediumship duties, each in his or her own style. Sometimes they would use billets, or pieces of paper on which the seeker's name and some sort of inquiry had been written—something, anything, it didn't matter what because they weren't going to read it. It was all about vibration. The medium would pull a billet from the basket, hold it in his or her hands for a moment to connect with the energy, then voila! Spiritual Western Union was open for business.

On my third visit, the sudden but staunch idea came over me that I wanted to receive a message—from whom or what and why, I did not know, but I went ahead and submitted my billet. Right before the reverend called my name, I had an electric sensation shoot up and down my spine. It was my great-grandmother talking to me—energetically at first, then verbally as relayed by the kindly man on stage. She talked about how I was always extremely curious from a young age, opening up every door, nook and cranny, looking in and checking everything out, and how she got a big kick out of me (as opposed to some others, who probably just wanted to kick me. At least I wasn't the kind of kid who asked a million needling questions; I was going to figure it out for myself come hell or high water.)

She encouraged me in specific ways, and assured me that I really was making a difference and bringing light into people's lives. She said I would be free of all negativity in another few years, and that it was going to be smooth sailing from here on out. What a soul-salve that was. The timing could not have been more perfect. Words cannot accurately convey the depth of feeling and meaningfulness I experienced. So sweet was the energetic transmission that I burst into joyful tears. That was probably the only church moment I've ever had that qualifies as a religious experience.

I really liked these Spiritualist characters. It's such an interesting cross-section of the populace that gravitates to their enclave. Many of them were old enough to be beyond the petty squabbles of life, and they were setting stellar examples for the rest of us. It was a weird social scene to be sure, but I found it comforting. People were friendly, perhaps wrapped up in their own life challenges at times (but then who isn't?), yet rarely ever showing even a smidgeon of judgmentality. After the Sunday service they held a caffeine-and-sugar social upstairs, and on special occasions, a full-blown potluck feast. Sometimes they'd be raffling off a handmade quilt or canning jars full of homemade jam. I'm a sucker for that kind of quaintness, so I took these opportunities to mingle with the regulars and eat some tasty vittles. And I love volunteering at events like theirs because I can be productive while buzzing around and socializing. It felt as if the community would always be there with open arms and no strings attached, no matter how long I stay away.

The old-timers had been brought up through the church under the tutelage of its esteemed founder, a powerful woman who was incarnate from 1892 to 1970. The reverends often mentioned her in their talks—clearly she was deeply revered and irreplaceable. But they seemed backward-looking, dutifully carrying out routines prescribed by a now-defunct era, and it felt a little sad. What was to become of the Church? Probably a few dozen church-goers held official memberships, but it seemed that no one ineligible for an AARP card was stepping up into any kind of leadership role. And if there was a new younger crop of inspired Spiritualists, would the program be updated for the times? That was a chicken-egg conundrum, as it appeared that revamping might be required to attract the fresh recruits in the first place. But these are just my own ponderings; the Spiritualists themselves were ostensibly unconcerned.

There was also an early morning Lyceum service, so naturally I checked that out too. It was more or less the equivalent of Sunday school, but there hadn't been any children in attendance for over eight years. Still, the reverends showed up every week and went through the motions, continuing to carry that torch. With an actual live interested human suddenly in their midst (that would be me), they seemed to scratch for material, then ad-libbed from a fallback list of tried-and-true subjects. Then they played a recording of a now-deceased church member channeling a Native American entity named Moonface. When it was happening real-time in the 1980s it was undoubtedly very exciting stuff, but from what I could hear of the scratchy old tape, Moonface wasn't divulging any ground-shaking insights by today's standards. I figured they just hadn't had a good channeler since. The only other person present, besides me and the reverends, was the elderly and mostly mentally-checked-out widow of the channeler. When they pushed "play" on the boombox, her entire being came to life. She listened intently, probably more to the energy and timbre of her late beloved's voice than to the content, as it was barely intelligible to those with unimpaired hearing. That heart-rendering scene quickly answered the question of why they would bother to maintain an otherwise senseless tradition.

Potentially tragic as it all seemed, it was fascinating to me that these elders were steeped in the paranormal.* I was enthralled with the idea that the 1920s and '30s—when my new friends had been young and impressionable—was an era of unprecedented widespread interest in woo, at a time when televisions and Facebook and all manner of electronic distractions did not yet exist. I wondered what it was like to take part in a séance in those days, or to be friends with the likes of Edgar Cayce and Arthur Ford. Perhaps I *had* lived a life there,

---

* The head reverend quietly informed me one day that the paintings on the walls were *spirit paintings*, not created by human hands. Oh, how I would've loved to see that in action!

in another human body—or maybe it was all happening right now? So many questions, so few answers. I wished that my great-grandma would talk to me about metaphysics from the other side... but I reckon that's just not her style.

5

Of Mormons and Daemons

"I asked for water and they gave me
rosé wine, a horse that knows arithmetic
and a dog that tells your fortune."
♫ Elvis Costello

One of my more "out there" friends was very excited about a modality she'd recently discovered called Theta Healing. At the time, its claims seemed pretty outrageous to me. There was matter-of-fact talk about altering DNA. You can't do that... *can you?* I was being ushered straightaway to one of my intellectual walls. In my limited academic exposure to biology, I'd latched on to the (apparently erroneous) idea that DNA was a static thing, a done deal, a sealed envelope. It wasn't up for negotiation, period, let alone alterable by the power of mere thought and belief. Still, I was intrigued, and more interested in finding out what lay on the other side of the wall than in re-mortaring the old bricks, so I suspended disbelief and moved forward—well, detoured around it is probably more accurate. I was beginning to grasp that just because I don't understand something, that doesn't necessarily make it untrue. Eventually... slowly, I would come to see that yes, Virginia, there *is* a DNA edit button.

My friend gave me the name of a certified Theta Healer who lived several hours away, so I rang her up for a phone appointment. To my surprise, she answered and we ended up having a mini-session right then and there. I didn't give her any particular complaints or issues to work on, but made it a let's-just-see-what-happens kind of thing. She didn't seem to need any fodder from me anyway, as she was one of those self-propelled frantic conversationalists.

The free heroin worked: I wanted more! That night and all through the next day, I couldn't help but notice—because I'd been such a shallow breather—that my breathing had deepened significantly. So I opted for a full hour-long session with her, during which fantastical beings and imagery appeared (well, to her anyway). She narrated all the while, bringing me along on the magic carpet ride in her mind. Wow. Little etheric helpers were purportedly all around me, extracting microbes from my blood and a giant crystal from my ear, among other things. She would pause for station identification periodically, working with me verbally to alter my core beliefs in some beneficial way. She told me of a spirit guide who's been tooling around with me since the get-go; he had an ancient Egyptian name. Oh, that and... the part where he and I belonged to the Brotherhood of Light from Sirius. Seriously? Would they let a sister into that club? I was both intrigued and incredulous.

I have to admit, I thought the woman was a little touched in the head. But then again, some of the most gifted and talented people *are* just that; being "normal" rarely produces anything extraordinary. So who was I to pooh-pooh the existence of angels, faery-creatures and moldy old disembodied star-pals? I figured the visual (or auditory, kinesthetic, etc.) interpretations people get are personalized. Energy appears to each person, or is translated, in such a way that somehow appeals or makes sense to him or her. I didn't want to automatically discount her ability to effect powerful healing. Something was definitely up with her though, because I never could get a hold of her afterward, nor did she ever charge my credit card for her work. Maybe she up and died or something? People do it all the time.

Well at any rate, she had given me a free ticket to a zany and thought-provoking show. I looked up the "brotherhood" and found some imaginative lore about reptilian conspiracies, dimensional shifts, blue lodges, pyramids, spirals... oh my. I was at a loss where to mentally file the stuff. So I didn't. It just seemed too wacky and abstract to warrant further study, and I've never been much of a sci-fi fan.

⚡ ⚡ ⚡

Still pretty excited and mystified by the healing potential, I decided to take a Theta Healing class myself. According to the almighty Interweb, the next one that fit my schedule was going to be held in Utah in a bedroom community of Salt Lake City. The instructor, Brenda, replied to my inquiry with lightning speed, and continued to contact me many more times before the event, providing this or that detail in small bursts, rather than a comprehensive FAQ of some sort. This was my first clue that something was amiss.

I'd driven through Utah many years ago, but I was on a mission to relocate from one coast to the other so I hadn't indulged in any leisurely touring. This time I allotted myself a few extra days for exploring, because the Rockies are always a treat and Utah has more than its share of natural splendor. Of course, I also had to check out that giant blue thing on the map.

The Great Salt Lake was nothing short of sublime. A truly majestic sight for sore eyes, its soupy layers of pale blues and pinks made it nearly impossible to discern sky from water; you had to do it from spatial memory alone. Linear distance was sheer trickery as well, for the waterscape spanned beyond accurate optical calculation—and probably into incalculable places and portals for all I knew. It wasn't hard to see why Brigham Young decided to pull up the horses and call it the Promised Land.

The workshop was held in Brenda's apartment, and there was only one other student. I paid the fee in cold cash which I'm sure did not get reported on any IRS form (not that I blame her). She gave us thick manuals and copies of the founder's book, which was a pretty rough cut and probably published in some stubbornly independent manner because the binding reads in the opposite direction of every other book I own. This founder apparently came up from the lower socioeconomic reaches of rural America when, in her time of greatest suffering, she was touched by God and experienced miraculous healing. Since then she's become the empress of this "new" healing method. I've heard rumors that she specializes in changing her celebrity clients' hair and eye color—a pretty wild idea, and a lucrative one at that. I'd love to witness such a thing firsthand. It would be deeply belief-shattering, not to mention a real hoot.

At first the workshop went swimmingly. I liked my fellow student Kay, a pleasant sixty-something Mormon woman who lived an hour away. I was starting to build confidence in my psychic abilities. We took turns closing our eyes and performing mental "body scans" on each other. I called out what I was "seeing" and those things turned out to be surprisingly accurate: neck pain, pancreas trouble. In my mind's eye, I saw the troubled areas of the body as being pronounced or lit up. In the case of the organ, its iconic shape was well defined and the word "pancreas" was spelled out across it in block letters, almost like a flash card. Thanks, spirit helpers! (They knew I hadn't taken anatomy classes.)

The basic gist of Theta Healing is that the person facilitating the healing is operating in a theta brainwave state, and this allows the magic to happen. Scientists who, for decades, have been strapping electrode contraptions onto people can attest to the fact that theta is a relaxed uber-state of consciousness. Sounds good, but how do you get there? A rather simplistic approach: after grounding yourself (for defying curfew, shame on you) you imagine going up through the 5th and 6th dimensions, on into the 7th Plane. Apparently that's where it's at, where they keep the *Creator* energy: a white sparkly place (seventh heaven?). So, it's a meditative procedure that happens very swiftly and leaves you wondering if you could possibly be "in" that special "place" and whether it could all really be so simple. I could have used a lot more time to practice, but Brenda was a bit manic in rushing us through the curriculum.

It was exciting stuff. Simple yet powerful. I was beginning to learn (or re-learn) that intention reigns supreme, and that outward efforting and striving, rowing against the current, really does not make things happen faster or better—more often than not it only impedes the desired results.

During a typical exercise, I would get in the theta zone, so to speak, then ask prescribed questions about core beliefs and maybe *command* a thing or two. Initially that word struck me as bossy and biblical, and I got a little twitchy when I heard it. But it's a team effort, this me-n-god thing. Brenda pointed to the "co" in "command." Even if I'm making a command, I'm getting the ideas downloaded to me first. It's important to remain open to answers, she said, as they come from outside the conscious mind. There is an emphasis on "god" as the healer, and we the healing facilitators as go-betweens or conduits. There's a lot more to be said about the subject, but basically it all hinges on having the audacity to believe you are powerful enough to talk with and co-create with god. And I say "god," meaning whatever higher power you like, although I was under the impression that Theta Healing was mildly Christian-flavored. I'm not sure why. Maybe it was their liberal use of words like "prayer" and "genesis." Not that it matters.

On one of our short breaks, I went to use Brenda's bathroom and noticed a picture on the wall that looked kind of like cherubs in space (not Pigs in Space—that's something entirely different). When I came back, she pointed to the wall hanging and rather assuredly told me that it had some connection to my energy, that I was from way, way, WAY on the outskirts of the galaxy, and that I had done this energy healing work before (and she didn't mean last month). Oh-kaaaay.

Although the basic procedure was rote, there was a wide assortment of tricks, tips, and applied projects in the manual. One of the exercises was designed to remove unwanted spirits or entities from a person or an area. You know... misguided souls, daemons without a cause, wayward phantoms, Lost Lester, Casper's evil twin. I really was not buying this one at all, thinking it sounded like old-fangled fear-based hoo-ha from the days of pagan witchcraft, but I went through the motions and did the thirty-second drill as instructed. When I opened my eyes, I was astonished—as was Kay—at the palpable change in the room. We looked at each other in wide-eyed amazement. The room felt lighter, brighter, and somehow transformed, and we each felt physically energized compared to the post-lunch food comas we'd been in less than a minute ago. Had we been unwittingly hosting some spiritual cling-ons, or was the instructor (or perhaps her apartment) responsible for luring them in?

Wow. This was the stuff made-for-TV movies are made of. The kind of project that normally requires hiring a specialist— probably someone who dresses bizarrely and exists outside the fringes of society—to come in and chase the unholy spook out of your house with lots of clanging contraptions and smoke and talismans and hullabaloo. And yet there we were, two ordinary women sitting calmly on the sofa, quickly and effectively performing some sort of mini-exorcism with all the action taking place in our imaginations. I could not have predicted that in a million years. And I probably wouldn't have believed it either, if I hadn't experienced it directly.

A few other exercises were interesting but none was as showy as that. Some were just plain boring. So much material was packed into this little weekend workshop that I really felt like I was getting my money's worth. But there was no way we could come close to covering it all. Part of the problem was that Brenda utilized too much time in personal storytelling. These were not stories you wanted to hear. Who wants to be privy to the intimate emotional, social, and medical woes of someone you've just entrusted and paid to teach you about healing? The more she droned on, the more evident it became that this was a lonely, broken woman before us (yes, living with her cats) and she was using her little captive audience for therapeutic venting. I didn't doubt for a minute that Brenda had special gifts, but I wondered why she hadn't applied them to herself more earnestly. She was a mess. Kay was squirming a little, and I was starting to run out of pity cards.

For lunch breaks, Brenda insisted that the three of us dine out together. That was fine by me because I was unfamiliar with the area and so far I'd only spied one unappetizing chain restaurant after another. All through lunch Brenda rattled on, continuing with the lesson plan—which was kind of awkward in a public setting. She clearly wasn't going to allow us any downtime of our own.

When we finished eating, I popped in an adjacent store in the strip mall to buy some tea—an errand which took all of two minutes to complete. Then it was back to Brenda's place, and we kept going into the early evening. Kay and I were both fairly exhausted by the time she let us go. When we returned the next morning, Brenda began discussing the day's schedule, and this time she wanted to extend the day even more. Kay and I instinctively protested, and with this Brenda launched into a tirade about how I had made us late yesterday and screwed up the entire schedule. Geez, this woman was even more of a nutter than I thought.

On the way to lunch this time, Brenda must have been feeling more comfortable with me and Kay, because she generously shared her right-wing political views with us. I said nothing and Kay took up the slack with a lot of polite "uh huh"s. While we ate, Brenda directed us to perform body scans of other restaurant patrons. Kay reluctantly complied but I refused to participate, as I wanted to simply eat in peace, but also because I found it unethical to just "scan" someone without their permission. Anyway, how would we even confirm what was accurate? What was the point? I understood that the small class

57

size limited the variety we could experience, but this was just too weird. Really it was a guise under which Brenda attempted to maintain control and, regrettably, Kay was her pawn in the charade.

At the close of the workshop, Brenda asked me about lunch — she at least had the sense to not make a scene in the restaurant, but I suspect that was only because it would not have served her control needs. Since she asked me point blank, I gave her an honest response. I let her know that I felt she had gone too far and violated boundaries. And it was a big drag too, because we came there to work in an altered meditative state, rendering us energetically vulnerable, and essentially she had shown herself to be irresponsible and unworthy of that trust. My candor catalyzed a huge blow-up on her part that transmuted to sulking and then finally ignoring me altogether as I took my certificate, bid her farewell, and left the building.

⚡ ⚡ ⚡

Unlike some of the other healing methods I've studied and researched, Theta Healing didn't seem to have much in the way of consistency or stringent requirements for certification, so probably this lack of accountability makes it a magnet for off-kilter personalities. Certainly Brenda was one of those, as was that first practitioner I worked with over the phone. Now, that's not to say that everyone involved with Theta Healing is nuts — that would be an error of logic, of course. All I'm saying is that if a person *is* crazy, and wants to pursue a certificate in energy healing, no one's going to screen them out if they choose Theta Healing. Seriously, though, I've since learned of at least one very sane, very effective practitioner out of New York City, and I'm sure there are many more reputable ones out there like him.

Kay emailed me afterward to thank me for speaking up and standing my ground with Brenda. She said she'd felt the same way but was unable to voice her opinion. I'm guessing her life experience had provided her with many solid years of submissiveness training. And there I was, playing the role of renegade again. Sometimes we typecast ourselves like that.

↯ ↯ ↯

After the workshop, I practiced Theta Healing a little bit with friends, but it wasn't long before I was drawn to the next shiny object, and like anything else, if I don't use it, I lose it. Perhaps I was destined to be a Jill of all woo games, master of none. But mastery can be overrated, if it's even attainable.

What I have used the most, however, is that mini-exorcism trick to clear out questionable energies when I stay someplace new like a hotel room. Ideally, this would be a routine pre-emptive activity, but mostly I forget to do it until the need becomes obvious. In one such instance, my friend Yoko and I were taking a road trip through Southern Oregon and had planned on tent camping, but it started pouring so hard that we decided to rent a yurt in one of the lovely coastal state parks. We settled in and went to sleep on the futons, but I awoke shortly thereafter, having experienced a very dark and disturbing nightmare. Interestingly, I was lucid in the dreamstate and recognized my urgent need to bust out of that reality, so I consciously woke myself up. I hadn't had a nightmare since I was a kid, so I knew it was something, or *someone's* weird energy in there 'cuz it sure wasn't mine. I hadn't thought to do any energy clearing before I fell asleep, but now, sitting up wide awake and spooked in the middle of the night, I was extremely motivated.

I employed the Theta method and threw in a few other energy tricks I'd picked up along the way from Lisa French and others, concentrating and visualizing as I meditated. After a few minutes, it felt noticeably better in the yurt and I was able to get back to sleep. I slept through the rest of the night with only my usual pleasant dreams. Seemingly impervious, Yoko was out cold through the entirety of it. Maybe the weird energy was localized, relegated to my side of the room—a task reserved for me in our division of labor. As a fire sign, she was good at making the campfires and burning stuff, and as an air sign, well, I suppose clearing the air was my job.

Who knows how these things work, really? All I know is that by doing the thing with a certain degree of authority, I was able to get results. It underlines the sheer power of belief. Believe, *really believe*, and it is so. That's about all there is to it, believe it or not.

6

MOVIN' TO THE COUNTRY
PART ONE

"What you once were isn't
what you wanna be… anymore."
♫ Wilco

The time had come for me to leave my city-home of ten years running. I didn't exactly have a plan. Actually, I had lots of them—moving to Hawai'i; joining a hippie commune; working on a cruise ship; attending full time woowoo school and becoming a bonafide energy healer; playing the full-on traveling vagabond musician; going to England for mediumship training; moving to a random American small town with an operative train station, getting a second floor apartment in an old-fashioned commercial district and taking a grocery store job; doing an organic farm apprenticeship; living in a treehouse. Those are just the ones that come to mind. I would adopt a new vision every few days and in the process, lose momentum and faith in the other mutually exclusive schemes. I was spinning my wheels and exhausting myself in mental expenditure. I didn't know where I was going, but just knew I had to *leave*. Blaming my immediate environment for the discomfort and lack of direction in my life seemed like the reasonable thing to do.

Besides, the city wasn't feeling so homey anymore—though not for any lack of homies on the streets. Even though I'd experienced noticeable relief after migrating from Bullet Central to a quieter family-oriented 'hood, things were starting to feel a bit weird and dark there too. Like... having some freaky person yelling at me while I was just minding my own business walking down the street. Often that person was my next-door neighbor, gone off his meds. One day he pulled a gun on his brother, who also lived on the block, and the cops came. It was beginning to feel like I'd landed in the middle of Hatfield and McCoy territory.

My street had undergone a radical transformation during the two years I lived there. Tearing apart and rebuilding my own little purple palace, I was a conspicuous element of change. Only, the rest of the block was moving in an entirely different architectural direction. Old craftsman beauties were being demolished and replaced with modern skinny ramshackle ones, two or three to the lot, as part of the city's nod to densification. During an estate sale, I had the privilege of going inside the most glorious of the old homes before it was annihilated. Or maybe it was an unfortunate occasion, because when the giant implements of destruction arrived, I felt the ache of it deep down inside, as if splinters of my soul were being extracted and hucked in the dumpsters alongside the old growth Douglas Fir and beveled glass built-ins. The felling of some huge stately old trees only rubbed salt in the wound. For a city that prided itself on being progressive and green, it didn't seem to see those loopholes coming. Or maybe it did, in back-room deals with developers, and I'd been naive in thinking otherwise. I was feeling disenchanted after my long extended honeymoon with Portland, but a decade is a pretty good run for someone with gypsy blood in her veins.

My house was my canvas, but alas, an immoveable one. I ended up creating some pretty fantastical stuff there. Friends would often stop by to ogle the many unique nooks and crannies, give mini-tours to other friends, or lend a hand with some large scale labor-intensive project. I was quite pleased with my creations, and had derived great pleasure from the quirky re-purposing of scrounged materials that I'd pulled out of dumpsters and roadside free piles. Bricolage had become my artistic specialization, and people were routinely blown away by the intricate detail and originality of the designs, often insisting that widespread publicity was in order.

As excruciating as it was to leave that wonderland behind, it almost felt like I had no choice in the matter, as if the urgency of change was some ginormous unstoppable boulder capable of crushing everything in its path, with my attachments becoming drawn out like taffy to a mere flimsy piece of twine that snapped under the weight of the thing. For a while I held on futilely to the severed cord, looking on in horror at its demise like a child whose prized kite had just been plundered by the elements.

What helped tremendously was that I'd been through the process once before. And this more recent detachment didn't require the use of external violence from the universe, thank god.

My previous house had been an even bigger ugly-duckling-turned-masterpiece. I thought I'd never leave that place; I used to joke about being carried out feet first. But when a rock sailed through my bay window one night narrowly missing my head, not too long after bullets had pierced the front window and scudded clear across the living room, my little joke nearly became reality. I heard the rock's wake-up call and didn't linger to push the snooze button. Hurriedly, I finished the renovations and put the house on the market. Four solid years of blood, sweat, tears, and tremendous creative energy had gone into it. This was no Home Depot remodeling job. Only a madwoman painstakingly hand-plasters entire walls and ceilings—so she can feel the sanctity of old-timey ways and press plants into the surface texture for copper-leafing—when a normal person just slaps up the sheetrock and mud and calls it good. Then again, I never dreamed I'd be handing over the keys to a stranger.

There is much to learn from letting go. I started thinking about that genre of art that's designed to be taken back by nature. I had to make the *process* the most enjoyable part of it rather than the end product. Still, there was a grieving period (and I was surprised, when I looked at the photos a year later, that it still hurt an awful lot). But unlike losing a person to death, it had been my personal choice, so clearly I had to consciously decide to release my attachments. When my outraged friends called to tell me the new owner had flippantly torn out nearly every shred of my handiwork, I couldn't allow myself to get too distraught for long. Besides, something freaky-cool happened. I hung up the phone, momentarily in shock, then noticed my CD player was malfunctioning—or so it seemed. It wasn't set on "repeat," and yet it was replaying the same song. Mathew Sweet sang: "I tried to hang on to the past, but I couldn't keep my grasp because nothing lasts."

I thanked the spirit-DJ out loud. "I get it! I honestly get it." The stereo then resumed its normal functioning.

⚡ ⚡ ⚡

With my newly feng shui-ed house sitting pretty on the market, I decided to split town and embark on a new set of hippie wandering adventures. It was summertime and I wanted out of the city in a big bad way. Swimmin' holes were calling! It was much easier to keep the house looking sharp for showings when no one was living in it, and that included my little feline housemate. Some friends of a friend had taken a shine to her, and so I found myself reluctantly giving her up for adoption. I knew she was better off with them; I had become an unfit mother. And I was far more attached to her than she was to me. I was definitely sad, though not nearly as melancholy as I would feel about it for years to come, after the dust settled. For the time being though, I had me a southbound train ticket and was excited about all the potentials an untethered life might hold.

The idea of living in an intentional agricultural community was very appealing—enjoying the beauty and expansiveness of raw acreage while sharing the work of maintaining it. I was prone to thinking about the inevitable implosion of the monetary economy, so being able to grow food and live off the grid were two highly coveted goals. Since I wasn't hooked up, joining a larger group seemed like the only way I was going to get in on this sort of scheme any time soon.

In a larger sense, I'd been holding onto the same dream of "living on the land" for nearly two decades, beginning with my married days (my ex-husband was quite the green thumb). Post-divorce, the grand dream had slowly morphed into a bunch of friends going in on land together to create a new utopian (though we never used that word) community. We held regular meetings and actually went to check out some properties for sale. After a while it became plain that each person or couple was in it for wildly different reasons. Some wanted a self-sufficient chosen-family farmstead as I did; others were seeking a recreational base camp. Some insisted that we'd need weapons and fences to protect ourselves and our resources; others were opposed to keeping animals on the property. You think you know a person until you try building a hippie commune with them.

Ever the optimist, I decided to explore another option: joining a well established community. If I could just find the right one where everything was perfect, I'd plunk down some serious dough, and they'd be ecstatic and use the money to buy new solar panels and stuff. Oh, and of course, I'd want to build my own house on the property. I'm not *that* community-minded, mind you. I envisioned a deep-green straw-bale beauty, entirely free of toxic materials and optimized for passive solar design. Eco-building and permaculture were my new focus and I acquired a modest armada of books on cob and straw-bale construction, earthen plastering, rainwater catchment, greywater recycling, composting toilets, gardening, and growing fruit, nuts and grains. I was ambitious and eager to get my hands into some dirt.

A friend of mine had been living and working in an intentional community in the Sierra Nevada foothills, so I decided to pay him a visit and have a look around. What I found there was a phenomenally beautiful and sizable piece of property... occupied by a very dysfunctional group of people. The land was graced with year-round creeks that flowed heartily past colossal chunks of granite and on down through a few glorious swimming holes—this in a particularly dry region of California. There were miles of hiking trails with spectacular views and wildlife, and a lovely little garden which my friend helped tend to earn his keep. The structures included some small dwellings—a funky bermed house, a strawbale, a geodesic dome —plus a composting toilet outhouse, garden sheds, and a 1970s bi-level that served as the group facility.

I sat in their group kitchen for hours, talking with whoever wandered in to cook and eat. Many of them griped about others who were not in the room, but failed to engage directly in conversation with them when they were present. Some of the clashes stemmed from the predictable problems of adults sharing a kitchen—different styles of organization, different standards for cleanliness—the stuff of twenty-something housemate drama. But these people were well into their forties and fifties, some with kids of their own, and I could not understand for the life of me why they would want to torture themselves this way. Perhaps they felt morally satisfied in owning just one seventh of a frying pan or a spatula? I really don't know. Some of their grievances had to do with bigger issues—actually, the really big stuff like what they were doing with their co-owned land. They seemed trapped on an endless hamster wheel trying to reconcile the irreconcilable and make each other change in accordance with their own specifications, and probably all the while thinking that with seven co-owners of a rural property, they were all but destined to stay there for the remainder of their days or else commit real estate suicide.

Needless to say, that visitation didn't exactly bolster my faith in communal living. I left with a sigh of resignation and a bevy of depressing thoughts about humankind, and made no further efforts to research intentional communities. Instead, I decided to pay a visit to a woman I knew who'd relocated from Oregon's big city to a tiny town just north of the California border.

⚡ ⚡ ⚡

Williams, Oregon bore a close resemblance to heaven. With true wilderness nearby, it had lots of space—both physically and psychically—and lovely evergreened mountainsides just teeming with wildlife. And there was garden-fresh and even hunted-and-gathered food, plus quaint dirt roads to amble down. I was in puppy love, caught up in the romantic notion of a woodstove-heated country lifestyle. After a few enchanted days there I returned to the city, but not for long, as I was magnetically drawn southward again to that obscure little dot on the map. It wasn't much to speak of really. The town itself consisted only of a general store, a post office, and not much more. But for some reason I found it irresistibly charming.

I didn't know Renée very well when she'd lived in Portland. In fact, our friendship had gotten off to a rocky start. Initially I avoided her when she appeared on the social scene because she just seemed phony to me. I couldn't tell who she really was, and I wasn't interested in doing the social excavation work to find out. So it was odd that, in this new time and setting, we were becoming fast friends. The icebreaker came when I heard that she was into energy healing— something we could bond over. I decided to try genuinely connecting with her. Maybe I'd been too hasty in my earlier assessment.

She responded by warmly and generously sharing her home and social circle with me. We were suddenly a couple of long lost sylvan sisters, laughing, cooking, eating, gardening and playing music together. And exchanging our woowoo knowledge. I discovered that she was a very powerful medicine woman, trained by Native Americans with whom she shared a bloodline. She normally kept this part of her life under wraps, so it was an honor to be privy to it. Finally, I could see beneath the misleading facade, and what I saw was simply amazing.

Back in the city, my house finally sold after a near deal-killing run-in with a wacky appraiser. The buyers' tenacity proved to me just how much they loved the house and all the work I'd done. Astrologer Bill had predicted such a turn of events, explaining that even though I listed the house in June and wanted to sell it pronto, there would be some sort of problem, and it wouldn't actually sell until September. He'd also said something disconcerting about me moving to the country—that I would uncover a fundamental weirdness... eventually. Hmmm. Sometimes it's better to go forth into the future blindfolded.

I moved my material possessions down to Williams, and Renée helped me find a nice place to live. I was blissed out. I had far more money in the bank than I'd ever had in my life, and no responsibilities whatsoever. I was feeling downright Abundant and pregnant with possibilities (not with a tiny human, thank goodness). One bright sunny day I was sitting on the ground under a shade tree, just basking and loving Life, appreciating the adorable little farmers' market when something shiny caught my eye in the dirt. I loosened the dirt surrounding it and was astonished to extract—in a grand gesture of the Law of Attraction—a solid gold bracelet! Renée seemed rather peeved at my good fortune, but covered up her displeasure with platitudes. It was another one of those times when the mismatch was painfully obvious between a person's words and the distinct vibe I was picking up. But I was just too dang happy at the time to dwell on it.

Meanwhile, I had discovered EFT—the Emotional Freedom Technique—which involves tapping certain points on the body that correspond to acupuncture meridians while reprogramming the subconscious mind. It's sort of an East-meets-West healing modality. You look and sound really stupid while you're doing it, but, hey I'm not proud. Apparently it had been wildly successful in helping veterans overcome their post-traumatic stress disorder without drugs. Not that I had anything to be stressed about myself. I was just curious as usual, and figured I'd try it in a proactive way.

I found a talented practitioner named Marelon Bjorkaes (who also happened to be an excellent astrologer) and we had a phone session in which I did the tapping on myself based on a diagram she'd sent me. She would ask questions that got to the heart of the matter, crafting the verbiage in just the right way, and these I would repeat after her when prompted. What makes EFT so powerful, I think, is that it's a dynamic process acknowledging changes as you go along. For example, "even though I *still* believe X, I now choose Y." It's all about keeping it real, and the subconscious mind seems to like that. The tapping, subtle as it is, can magically clear out stuck energy, in a sort of homestyle do-it-yourself version of acupuncture needles. And often with enormously positive results.

The subject I chose to focus on with Marelon was the ever popular boyfriend acquisition project. Largely unbeknownst to my conscious mind, I had some deep-seated beliefs that were staving off the mating season. I mean, besides the obvious. Sure, my emotional crisis-mode emanation had been acting as man-repellant—or maybe even a sledgehammer crushing all potential crushes within a thousand-mile radius—but then again, I had been more or less single for a whole decade before the Crisis came to town. Marelon used my astrology chart and her intuition to get down to brass tacks. Some of the stories on my internal newswire were: "there aren't any age-appropriate single men" and "all the guys around here are wusses" or "I will lose my independence if I get hooked up." Helpful stuff like that. So with her able assistance, I talked and tapped the crapola out of my circuitry.

A week later, I met a man who was cute, charming, about my age, interested and assertive enough to ask me out. That hadn't happened since, oh, I don't know, *ever*? And this was in that itsy-bitsy town in the country, against all statistical odds. I'd been living in a city of half a million people for years with very little action, then I rolled into Hooterville and had me a date before the end of the barbeque. Utterly astounding. Marelon had positively earned my praise and respect. It was a sweet little affair that endured for all of a month, at which time it was eclipsed by the next chapter in my romantic saga (more on that shortly).

I was so impressed with the power of EFT, I picked up a read-it-in-one-day paperback manual and also downloaded some free guides from the web.   The authors explained that many phobias and conditions of a psychological and/or physical nature can be cleared up —and often within seconds.   Well, I had a few phobias myself, as a matter of fact.   I was afraid of heights under certain conditions, though this didn't really interfere with the quality of my day to day life; I mostly considered it an asset of self-preservation.   But I had this other little problem.   For years I could not drive on the freeway without having a full-blown panic attack.   Living in the city without owning a car, this weirdness of mine hadn't caused much of a ruckus.   When I did drive, I would just stick to the back roads or city streets.   Usually someone else did the driving anyway, and that was just fine by me.   I'm not sure exactly when or why I developed the freeway anxiety, but I supposed it wasn't all that fruitful to ruminate on its origins.

With my back-and-forth city mouse/country mouse life unfolding, at one point I found it necessary to make a five hour road trip with a borrowed car.   Until then, I'd gotten rides, taken trains or buses, patched it together somehow.   But there was no getting around it this time.   I had to go retrieve my stuff—and soon—because the friend who'd been letting me store my things in her garage had a sudden change in priorities.   I still had a lot of tools and raw materials because I figured I'd be building an eco-house in the near future.

With nothing to lose but my panic attacks, I applied EFT.   I did a few rounds of it, then bravely set out for a test drive. Miraculously, everything was fine!   Then I embarked on the big trip. About an hour into it, I felt a mild version of the panic coming on, so I pulled over and did more EFT (there must have been a little residual "stuff" left) and that took care of it.   I've been driving calmly on freeways ever since: a total success story.

EFT probably works better for some things and certain people as opposed to others.   But it's just as likely that success hinges on how adeptly the tool is wielded.   It's definitely worth trying for anything that ails you, especially since you can do it yourself and without spending any money.   The only real risk is in looking ridiculous if someone happens to catch you in the act.

Of course there are people who annoy everyone around them by constantly talking about EFT and applying it to everything and anything. Which makes me think of that Mark Twain adage, "when all you have is a hammer, everything looks like a nail." Not everything's a nail, agreed, but when you do hit the nail on the head, there's no disputing it.

7

DELUSIONS, PART WON

"All our troubles, I know,
are mostly of our own design.
As for the love you gave me,
I'll keep it in mind."
♫ Ron Sexsmith

"We're sending you to a really good oncologist." Yikes. A straight dose of liquid terror shot up my spine. I remembered a silent vow I'd made to myself many years ago, that if ever I should come down with a cancer, I would use energy healing to take care of business. I sat stupefied by the pop quiz I'd just been dealt. Could I really walk that kind of talk in the face of such chilling news? My head was spinning as I half-listened to the gynecologist talking a little too enthusiastically about robotic surgery.

The sheer power of my own creativity was confounding. I'd managed to create an ovarian cyst bigger 'n Dallas that was suspected of harboring mutant cells and of being temperamental—they feared the thing might explode if they didn't get to it soon. Dammit, I just *knew* this had something to do with my mother.

I found myself suddenly swept into the medical-industrial complex with unprecedented acquiescence. I had happily kept out of it for most of my life because I'd generally been in good health, but also due to some ornery autonomous ways learned early on. My family went to doctors only on rare occasions, and usually because of some school requirement. We were like Christian Scientists, but without the Christianity or the science. My parents just had a no-nonsense approach to things, handed down through the lineage of hardscrabble Protestant folk. "Tough it out, kid" was the answer to anything short of life-threatening illness or injury, and hypochondria was usually met with dismissive laughter.

As a grown-up (if I dare call myself that), I'd gravitated to the teachings of Louise Hay and others who insisted that dis-ease is not random victimization or luck of the DNA draw, but rather, it has a psycho-energetic root cause and carries with it an important message. Theoretically, if I created the cyst in the first place, I could also dis-create it, but the task was daunting to say the least. Figuring out the "why" of things and actually transforming the situation are two entirely different projects—a little bit like learning to play *Twinkle Twinkle Little Star* versus a Chopin nocturne.

It seemed to me that most people treated their bodies like cars, taking them in to the mechanic for repairs—just looking to git'er fixed and not really wanting to be responsible for the inner goings-on. And the medical worker bees are mostly too harried to treat you as anything other than just another Ford or Subaru. It was very surreal, then, a week after I got that news, to be joining the masses in the human parking lot—the overly lit waiting room of the oncology building. What a cheery place it was. People stared like zombies at blaring televisions or else compared notes with each other about which grim procedure they were currently undergoing. Well, at least there was community in it.

When it was my turn to get five whole minutes of undivided personal attention with a surgeon, the white-coats swiftly ushered me in through the serpentine bowels of the facility. She was surprisingly young, overworked and overtired, this specialist who'd come so highly touted. Very casually, she explained the recommended procedure: they would remove both of my ovaries along with the menacing cyst, and while they've got me cut open like that, they would also like to take out the band of belly fat (well, *that* part might be nice, actually), and my uterus might as well go too. I was horrified! It sure sounded like a hysterectomy to me. She warned of a six-week recovery, because unfortunately the cyst was too large to send in their cool little robots. Drat. (Why is it that robots always let you down just when you need them?) The thought of being sliced, diced and julienned and then having to lay around in bed for a month was unfathomable.

Then, at the very end of the consultation she added *"or... you could just wait and see."* Yes! Breathing room. Wait and see. That was my Get Out of Jail Free card. Wait and see. That's what I would do. I would wait and apply all the woo-woo juju in the land, then have a re-test, and then they would see—we all would see—that the dreaded cyst was gone, gone, gone. Gone like a light-rail fare-snaker into the wilds of North Portland. Yup, that's what I was going to do, alright.

I walked around in a daze for another week or so, grappling with the conflicting ideas swirling around in my head. I knew, at the core of me, that energy and intention could resolve anything. But at the same time I was being heavily influenced by fear and mainstream thinking within and around me, and by one man in particular...

ϟ ϟ ϟ

It wasn't exactly love at first sight. In fact, the first time we allegedly met I had no recollection of it, as it was during one of my over-the-top theme parties, and I was busy socializing and putting out fires in typical hummingbird hostess fashion. The second time we met I had the distinct sensation of repulsion, of not even wanting to speak to him. It's not that Mike was inherently repulsive. It was an intuitive perception, that urge to run away, and a warning of things to come, perhaps based on some sort of karmic entanglement—or just plain old common sense.

But a certain cocktail of time, delusion, and hormonal mayhem has a way of erasing from conscious memory such wise assessments. I suppose I'd been hitting that sauce pretty hard because two years after meeting, there we were, living together and making big plans—and not getting along. The cyst that cropped up was a microcosm of the relationship: a thing that should not be, growing more ominous by the day.

The relationship started gathering steam when we found ourselves in close proximity traveling to and from southern Oregon to visit Renée. Mike lived in Portland, but after I moved to the country, his visits there became more inspired and more frequent. At first we were just friends, having lots of fun group adventures—hiking, camping, swimming, boating, partying. Or helping Renée around the homestead. We were a happy little brat pack—the three of us and a fourth male friend who had the hots for Renée.

Mike and I started sleeping together, and things changed rapidly. The physical attraction and chemistry was overpowering—as sex was our greatest area of connection—and it took over my brain like some kind of alien space pod. I went to visit him back in the city one weekend and I never left.

During the week he would go to work and I'd play '50s housewife and make dinner. The role-playing was pleasingly novel. Every weekend we'd embark on some fabulous road trip adventure with his dog. And that was a particularly beautiful thing, because I'd never been a "dog person" before. In fact, I really didn't want anything to do with the slobbering critters; I was a "cat person" through and through. But this particular canine was so lovable that he won me over in a matter of weeks and left me laughing at the fact that I'd once stated "I'll never date a man with a dog." Never say never.

A couple months later, emotional tumult barged right into la-la land. I'm sure it came as no surprise to our mutual friends who'd shown varying degrees of perplexedness and antagonism at our unlikely partnership. The thing that fastened us together, other than the sex and its resultant fledgling emotional bond, was our shared dream of having land in the country. We'd gotten together at a time when both of us were dissatisfied with the city life and longing for open space, fresh air, and free time to play in it. So we went looking at property to buy together, telling ourselves and each other that even if we were to break up, we could still be friends and members of the same community. Ri-ight.

A particularly candid friend looked me in the eye and said, "I think it's completely *insane* to buy land with someone you're not married to." Her words rang true, but not to the extent that they should have. My reaction was more like "ha ha! yeah, that's right, I'm insane."

So insane, as a matter of fact, that I was helping Mike remodel his house so he could sell it and buy land with me. My irrepressible need for a project had resurfaced. Things had been so copacetic in Williams—I had not a care in the world, and that was the problem: I needed an outlet for my energy, something or someone to focus on, to work toward. A log for a pit bull.

Lucky Mike. He had himself a live-in girlfriend who was also a project manager extraordinaire. I whipped that place into shape and took care of all the small details of procurement and contracting. But it was a perfectly equitable arrangement because I was living rent-free, and for the most part it was a labor of love. Evenings and weekends, we'd work on the house together—sometimes having fun, but increasingly we would argue. His lovely Craftsman home was being transformed into a big rumbling pressure cooker.

After the first contentious argument, I moved out. A friend of mine was away for the holidays so I had an easy place to stay. Sad and confused, I went for a tarot card reading. A local psychic named Patti had come highly recommended by a good friend of mine who was not particularly woowoo; she'd really blown his mind. My own reading was no less monumental. She seemed to peer right into my soul and tell me exactly what my life had been like since birth—such incredible validation. She laughed incredulously while remarking that I'd "asked for a high level of initiation" in this life. Maybe she was right, and I'd bitten off more than I could chew.

Our session went on for hours, but she charged me for a mere twenty minute reading. There was an immediate, strong sense of kinship between us. In fact, she told me she knew me from other lifetimes, one having been in a convent thousands of years ago. Hmmm...interesting. It's not that I doubted her, but I just didn't have that kind of recall. I felt a bit like the doofus at a party who doesn't remember someone with whom he's already spent quality time.

"Alright, so who *is* this Gemini guy?" She handed me a box of tissues. "Get rid of him! He's not *the one*!" With that missive, I started to lighten up, laughing through my tears. There was another man, she said—a real and proper match—waiting in the wings. He sounded amazing. Too amazing for me to believe, as much as I wanted to.

Patti imparted past life tales of me and Mike involving themes of unequal social roles and unrequited passion—these helped to explain the otherwise nonsensical attraction between us. Of course, I have no way of truly knowing whether these other lives existed (or exist) but the mission had been accomplished: greater clarity and emotional relief. I sauntered out of her spiritual apothecary altered, armed with the knowing that Mike was definitely, *absolutely*, beyond question and without a doubt, the wrong man for me. I had to move on.

I got myself a small apartment across town with a month-to-month lease. I just needed a little time on my own to regroup and devise a plan for getting myself back to the country. But where? Certainly not to Williams. My friendship with Renée had burned to the ground when she blew a fuse one day after a string of awkward communications. But it was just a matter of time. I could see how she'd been stockpiling an arsenal of resentments, and any spark would have set off that grenade.*

She wasn't the only one acting funny. I started seeing how the whole place had a strange vibe to it, because of the fact that marijuana growing was the main economic activity in the valley. Hey, I'm no square, but when partying turns to paranoia, it can be a real drag. I walked away from Williams without regret, albeit slightly rattled that astrologer Bill had predicted the plot twist, I guess because it implied that life is a bit more pre-ordained than I'd like to think.

What next? I knew I wanted to live in a small town near undeveloped land, so I started researching some cute towns in Oregon —Silverton for one, with its transgendered mayor (that fact alone spoke volumes about the open-mindedness of its citizenry). In the meantime, I was enjoying some unfettered quality time with city friends, and frolicking in the unusually sizable snowstorm that befell Portland that winter. And while I was playing and re-grouping, I was also tending to my ever-inquisitive mind.

⚡ ⚡ ⚡

Patti came from a long line of mystical folk of Theosophist flavor. I'd never heard of theosophy before meeting her, but curiosity led to my attempted reading of Helen Blavatsky's intimidating tomes. That woman had a seriously large cranium. She actually apologizes in the introductory pages for being a non-native English speaker, but I've never seen such an assiduous command of the language. (Then again,

---

* I learned something fascinating about gender roles after discussing the situation with my wise and observant friend Sheila. Renée had accused me, among other things, of being a terrible friend because I hadn't asked her about x, y, or z going on in her life. Well, I always figure that if someone has an update they will share it, but I'm not about to pry otherwise. I've got a strong aversion to interrogation-style conversation, so naturally I don't want to subject others to it either. Sheila explained that women tend to communicate in this fashion, drawing out the information from each other (and from the men) and that I was not like that at all; in fact Sheila herself had had an adjustment period when our friendship was getting off the ground. I suppose I'm more like a dude in that way—or perhaps an alien?

I'm something of a literary heathen.) "Why are we here?" and "How does it all work, this universe thingy?" are always compelling questions, but dumbing down the answers was, in this case, imperative. Fortunately, Patti had some paraphrased materials to lend me, and I acquired some Alice Bailey books as well, that gave me an inkling of the Theosophists' tenets.

As far as I can tell, theirs is a broad-minded approach, a mythos derived from ancient esoterica. The Theosophical Society was born in the late 19th century, making them likely amicable cohorts to my pals, the Spiritualists. The books describe a sort of master plan via very long phases of life and their pervasive themes like love and wisdom—far longer epochs than we humans are in the habit of examining. Hell, most of us are focused on tonight's drama at the dinner table.

Among other things, they talked about the consciousness (and expansion thereof) in the human, animal, plant, and mineral kingdoms. Wait, now, hold on just a minute—*conscious minerals*? Having gone through engineering school, I'd been well-imprinted with the habit of categorically separating the organic from the inorganic. It was simple sorting hinged on the presence or absence of carbon molecules: organic is "alive," inorganic is not. Certainly consciousness has something to do with being alive, right? I could easily conceive of animals having consciousness, and even plants, but... *rocks*? I had studied the intricate crystalline structures—obvious evidence of some kind of brilliant design—but that word *consciousness* in connection with minerals baffled me. I could not get my mind around it. So I stopped trying and continued reading and going about my life.

Eventually I understood that the problem lay in my rigid definition of consciousness. It happened sometime after my first Monroe Institute experience (more on that later). Apparently I had amassed enough related insight, or enough of a change in perspective, so that when someone remarked, "without consciousness, a rock would simply be a random set of molecules" something clicked. It may not be obvious in the words that triggered it, and it's not easy to articulate, but it was as if I suddenly understood that "spirit," if you will, was infused in rocks along with everything else. Not that I literally saw or felt anything, because I still didn't perceive "crystal power" as some others do. But I could at least entertain the concept for once. And it felt really good. Why is that? Maybe it's a releasing of burden, a relinquishment of responsibility for knowing. I started noticing that the more steps I took away from intellectual arrogance and toward a more childlike posture of intrigue and possibility, the happier I was.

⚡ ⚡ ⚡

Back in Dramarama-land, somehow, inexplicably, I began dating Mike again. The alien pod was back. Or maybe it'd merely been dormant while I enjoyed a sojourn from insanity. I'm not really sure how it happened. He would show up with flowers and take me out for dinner—kinda like Ike and Tina, without all the smacking. I moved back into his house, and we were back on the "let's buy land together" plan, this time in the Oregon coast range. Our friends shook their heads in grave disbelief.

Then came the breaking news of that ovarian cyst to thicken the misery-plot a bit more. My vow to start a vigorous energy healing regime quickly languished, and in an unconscious act of reversion to old patterns, I employed the trusty "ignore it" method of healing. I filled my mind instead with details of house remodeling projects. Part of me knew how very wrong it was to be working doggedly amongst particles and fumes while hosting a potentially cancerous time bomb in my belly. But I was on autopilot, doing what was familiar because it seemed easiest, and not wanting to stop and think about things that had no ready-made answers. Those alien pods run a tight ship.

I had this idea I was chewing on—that I was a quitter—and so I was determined to make the relationship with Mike work. When you get to be over forty and single for a while, crazy ideas can start running through your head—like second thoughts about a divorce that happened long ago, even though you know damn well it was the best decision you've ever made. The Neptunian mist was impairing my judgment, big-time. But only about ninety percent of the time, leaving a one-in-ten chance for pinholes of light to appear on any given day.

81

I'd been reading *A Return to Love* by Marianne Williamson and taking to heart the principles espoused in *A Course in Miracles*. I was genuinely trying to love Mike unconditionally, however awkward and futile an undertaking that was. Then I had a very poignant dream that told me in no uncertain terms that I was barking up the wrong tree. In my dream, there was a TV game show and I was a contestant. Before going on the air, I happened to witness an inside deal between two executives. One said to the other: "when we throw *this guy* in the mix, no one can win!" (evil laughter ensued). It was rigged, not unlike the movie *Quiz Show*. I went out and played the game, and I don't recall the specific question but my answer was obviously correct because it was displayed up in the trees (don't you just love dreams?) and the crowd cheered. Everybody could see it, everyone knew it was the right answer, and yet I didn't win. I could not win because *that guy* was there. Unconditional love was indeed the answer, but it was pointless for me to keep trying it with Mike.

We really did not understand each other, and were extremely adept at pushing each other's buttons without even trying. I had Marelon Bjorkaes do a synastry chart reading to get the relationship lowdown through the eyes of astrology. Not surprisingly, the report described a horrendous mismatch. There were a prodigious number of inter-aspects, many of them deeply magnetic, and most of them tragically impossible. Astrology need not be fatalistic, but when the truth is clearly laid out in front of you like that, it's difficult to stay in denial. She surmised that Mike was a very young soul, and the sentiment felt right, though I can't say I understood what it means. I mean, where do souls come from if they're new (or old, for that matter)?

Despite the clarity that was bubbling up, inertia took a few more months to overcome. When we finally broke up for good, I spent a few days swimming, and nearly drowning, in soul-wrenching grief. It was very painful, but not for the reasons one might think. I was faced with the stark cold reality that I had deceived and deluded myself—that I had derailed my life plan for an entire year because of fear. I had to finally admit to myself that while I did love Mike, I was drawn into the relationship for the wrong reasons. I didn't want to go it alone, so I'd found someone who claimed to have the same goals, and we both latched on to that false security. The pain was between me and myself, and had very little to do with him. It was the most intense mourning I've ever experienced. I was staring face-to-face at the fact that *I alone* was responsible for my life, for what I had created, what I would yet create, where and how I would live.

But there are only so many tears you can cry*. I started feeling better simply as a consequence of using up all the feel-bad molecules in my system. I'm glad I didn't attempt to palliate; the upheaval ran its course more quickly and completely that way. Stripped of my delusions, I had no other viable option than to gather up the remnants of my psyche and start looking around for the next soft landing. But then, I do like to have a project.

⚡ ⚡ ⚡

I never did go under the knife. My research revealed that ovarian cysts come and go, shrink and grow, and that the type of cyst I had was unlikely to be cancerous. A few groovy healers and psychically-attuned friends made assertions that my energy field did not contain the "cancer signature," and I chose to go along with those sentiments. I re-took the diagnostic tests. The cyst had shrunken a tiny bit by that time, and the blood data seemed okay, so that was enough encouragement for me to walk away from the mainstream medical world with some degree of confidence in my ability to heal. I figured if it hadn't gotten any worse with the stressful way I'd been living, then surely I could make it vanish under more favorable conditions. It seemed to me that the whole thing had been blown out of proportion anyway. I'd gone along with the brouhaha for a minute, as if getting sucked into some huge Suess-ian looking moneymaking machine, but thankfully emerged out the other side, mostly unscathed, wits relatively intact.

I decided what I needed most was respite in the country—a place with clean air, clean water, good food, and lots of time on my

---

* Sorry, I couldn't resist borrowing that Journey lyric.

83

hands to meditate and get to the bottom of this cyst business once and for all. In the meantime, new flavors of woo were beckoning...

8

REALITY IS NEGOTIABLE

"What you mean, that's what you get.
Did you forget to know
what the end is?"
♫ Sean Hayes

I figured it was going to be just another typical energy healing seminar—pretty sedate, probably New Agey, and perhaps a bit too touchy-feelie but I was getting kind of used to that. Maybe a few dozen people would be there. It was taking place in a hotel, which is a normal venue for this type of thing (when it's not being held in someone's living room, that is). I schlepped myself to the Seattle hotel via mass transit and was feeling ultra-low on energy, having come fresh out of boyfriend-and-cyst trauma land.

It came as a jolt to my system, then, to walk into a giant well-lit ballroom already packed to the hilt with hundreds of people cavorting and chatting. I managed to find a seat before the show began. And, oh what a show it was.

Music started blaring—familiar classic rock tunes on a kick-ass sound system. Then the guy—the dude, the emperor, the cult of personality—made his way through the crowd and up on stage, all the while laughing like a mad man and playing air guitar. He was flanked by two pretty blondes: a rock star fantasy in action. The majority of the audience was on their feet, some standing on chairs careening to see, nearly all of them goofily clapping along and buzzing with wild anticipation. It looked exactly like a religious revival tent, but with Marriott décor.

"Oh my god. What have I spent my money on this time?" If my friends could have seen me at that moment, I would have been *so* embarrassed. I think I was anyway. I had run away to join the circus and was having one of those "careful what you wish for" moments.

When the song ended and the cheering died down, Mr. Dude launched into an extended monologue comprised of pontifications on the futility and arrogance of modern medicine, hilarious accounts of bizarre personal experiences, and wild tangents about aliens, teleportation, parallel universes, invisibility cloaking, time travel, and shape-shifting. It took me a little time to realize that these were not actually tangents. This *was* the relevant content of the seminar—all of it.

Hands-on demonstrations were thrown in the mix, sometimes as spur-of-the-moment inspirations ("hey, you…come up here!") or in more formal examples en masse—for instance, all the people who suffer from a particular condition such as asthma, or all the engineers in the house (who suffer from intellectualism). Then there was a laying on of hands that resulted in the laying out of bodies. The stage became littered with carnage—some people were out cold for hours before re-emerging into consciousness. I don't know if that's the way Holy Rollers do it, but this gig was looking mighty evangelical... except the Rapture was supplanted by uproarious Laughter. The "victims" seemed completely blissed out, and some entered into convulsive fits of silliness. Later in the day, waves of hilarious contagion pulsated through the entirety of the room, and people were literally rolling on the floor, shrieking, snorting and contorting themselves, powerless to resist the pee-in-your-pants glee-surge when it struck. We were told this was the work of Frequency 16: the dolphin energy.

The larger-than-life character responsible for all this joyful mayhem was Dr. Richard Bartlett, founder and ringleader of Matrix Energetics (ME). A chiropractor turned naturopath turned metaphysical troubadour, this iconoclastic and magnanimous showman was about to teach me a thing or two about physics. And consciousness. And reality. Which, turns out, are all hopelessly intertwined. Things don't fall into well-behaved boxes the way we're trained in school. Take medicine, classic rock, and religious revivals, for instance—the boundaries are blurrier than you might think.

↯ ↯ ↯

It was fairly obvious that Bartlett's reality diverged wildly from what most people experience. Some very trippy things have happened to the guy, inspiring him to do a lot of research and hands-on experimentation and share the findings with others. They call ME a "consciousness technology" and I agree that it is distinctly different from mere healing modalities. It's not even focused on healing per se, although that's the big draw for most people. Everyone wants healing to occur, of course. But getting attached to outcomes and raising the stakes only creates an impediment to desired results. Lightening up and really playing with energy—*playing with reality*—is the antidote to over-analysis and doubt... and the key to manifesting weirdness.

Bartlett's tech talk made a lot of sense to me, despite (or perhaps because of?) his extra-colorful delivery. It was actually quite riveting, because he's a genuinely funny and likable dude. When he gets too crazy, that's where the ladies come in to balance him out and keep him on task—or just take him off task if need be. They turned out to be his girlfriend and daughter, and each proved to be wise and humorous in their own right, though for my money, not quite as entertaining as Bartlett himself (but those are some big shoes to fill). Perhaps the old adage is true that every comedian needs a straight man, so to speak.

I was no stranger to physics, but most of my academic exposure was of the Newtonian variety. I had recently jump-started my quantum re-education by finally reading that vintage paperback classic, *The Dancing Wu-Li Masters*, as well as a few others. Back in college, we did dabble in the quantum stuff, but I wasn't ready for it then (and in engineering school, they sure as hell weren't going to touch the mystical implications of it with a forty foot pole). When my physics professor had introduced gluons and quarks, I pronounced the whole thing "ridiculous" and refused to listen, just as I'd balked in high school algebra when they brought out the imaginary numbers. Which is all pretty shocking considering I was experimenting with mind-altering recreational substances in those days. I guess the expansion took its sweet time. I was very left-brained, and any concepts that didn't fit neatly into my black-and-white sorting mechanisms simply got rejected. There was no mind-file labeled "I'll just wait and see, and think about it later." What a long way I'd already come.

Meanwhile in the larger world, physicists have known and shown for over a century that reality has options. Whatever occurs is partially determined by who's observing it, so there is no such thing as one single absolute objective reality. Truly, reality is a subjective experience. And that's not just an abstract intellectual concept; it has practical implications for society. It explains, for example, why people squabble so much—they're not experiencing the same reality but they're totally convinced that they *ought* to be, so they repeatedly try to attain this elusive goal, usually by making other people wrong. Can't we all just get along and mind our own realities?

Long before the physicists started wising up, eastern mystics have been telling us that reality is but an illusion—a projection of the mind. It's just that our time-space environment, our experience of dense physical reality that we all mostly agree upon, is so damned convincing that it's difficult for us to consider—let alone comprehend —that it's all just a big holographic sandbox we're playing in here. Everyday life looks so solid and real and dependable... until someone like Richard Bartlett comes along and blows your mind by correcting a person's scoliosis right before your eyes. Or triggering a flood of pronounced emotion across the face of a previously hard-nosed stoic engineer. Both miracles in their own right.

Essentially, physics and mysticism are both saying there are infinite parallel realities to choose from at any given moment, and we are continually observing a refresh, a brand new version of reality all around us in each moment. It only *seems* the same because we've gotten so very skilled at maintaining consistency—so good at it, we don't even know we're doing it! And that's normally a beautiful thing. It *is* nice to come home and find your house in the same dimension, the same point on the grid where you left it, right? Consensus reality, or our consensual hallucination, is what keeps us in stasis. But as for me personally, I think stasis is a big boring drag. Well, I should clarify that. *Involuntary* stasis can feel like a straightjacket but involuntary chaos could be even worse. Ideally, there would be complete creative control with the option of "more of the same, please" or a complete change of scenery for every fork in the reality road encountered.

If you happen to have a broken leg, you might want to "step into" a radically different reality in the next moment, perhaps a different version of your life in which your leg is healthy and in fine working order. But then, you might find that your house is a different color or you're married to a different person. I don't know. All possibilities exist, if only we are able to cast off the shackles of consensus reality. A handful of humans have been known to do it— like those martial arts masters who break a solid piece of wood in half with just a slight blow of the hand, or the spoon-benders who walk amongst us, or those overnight-miracle cancer patients you sometimes hear about. It's a science of the mind, of the consciousness. But how on Earth does one get there from here?

⚡ ⚡ ⚡

Dr. Bartlett's exotic traveling show came to town with a well-stocked toolbox. He had lots of creative, fun ways of working with the imagination in order to (potentially) experience quantum leaps. The most basic tool is the "two-point method." It may not look like much to the casual observer, but here's the idea behind it: you select any two points—be they on a person's body, out in space, on a lampshade, whatever—it makes no difference where, *except* that the selection should come to you as an intuitive download, rather than a calculated left-brain action in order to be truly effective. You can either literally place your hands at those points or just imagine doing so. Next, you envision a continuous line of light between them.

This is where, by way of analogy, I like to employ 1980s computer graphics terminology. We normally think of reality as a collection of 3D vector graphics, meaning that every person or thing is a succinct object with easily identifiable boundaries. But in raster or bitmapped graphics, there is just a string (in 2D that is—in 3D it becomes a grid or a matrix) of pixels or tiny units of energy—some having the qualities of air, some of a desk, some of human flesh, etc. By no longer making a big distinction among the objects and their molecules, I could "blur" my perspective a bit and begin to loosen the stronghold my left-brain has had on my perception of reality. (Actually, observing and measuring is what the left-brain does best; when it pretends to be the masterminder, that's where we typically get into trouble.)

The next step in two-pointing is to "collapse the wave." But not before you "drop down into your heart," a nebulous but crucial step in the process. Coming from a right-brained, heart-centered consciousness is really the crux of the biscuit here; it's what allows the magic to happen. Presumably, it's a skill that comes more easily with practice.

90

Wave functions are a delightfully nerdy concept, but what's going on in practical terms is that you're imagining that line of light (or photons, or pixels, molecules, whatever) between the two points suddenly breaking up, leaving it all—the space, the molecules, the energy—free to re-form itself. Immediately after the collapse, you can send your conscious mind to the beach for a moment, or anything else that gets it out of the way temporarily. Then you are free to come back and *observe* reality again and notice if anything is different. Often it isn't, due to the aforementioned human inclination to sameness, but that doesn't disprove the theory. Old habits do die hard, but they can also be kicked with desire and a certain degree of dedication to change.

There are many ways to observe a changed reality—or to simply observe reality for that matter. Imagination knows no natural limits, just the ones we impose upon it. As a Matrix Energetics "practitioner," you might "see" a cartoon superhero coming to life, or a little bird that flies in and sits on the client's shoulder telling you what to do next. Or the client's face might morph into a machine with levers and buttons that you adjust (in your imagination) with surprisingly pleasing results. Dropping all judgments is key in allowing the creative process to flow in whatever unpredictable fashion it will.

In "working" (two-pointing, for example) with others—people, animals, objects—the idea is that there is quantum entanglement. Your molecules, their molecules, everything in between—it's all part of the reality you're perceiving, and is all, therefore, subject to change. It's a matter of taking conscious control of a process that we are constantly doing on an unconscious automatic basis. It's tricky, this brain balancing act, because even though you want to be conscious while you're doing it, *you* as a personality are really not in control. You want to be in a mode of noticing, being curious, observing, listening and waiting for information and then taking inspired action (although the "action" mainly exists in the mind's eye, so to speak). This is markedly different from the way most of us have been encouraged to operate. And while I understood all of this, I was still having a hard time because my monkey brain was reluctant to share the reins.

That "reset" of energy represented by the wave-collapse concept provides an explanation for why people often fall down or pass out at ME seminars: it's like the body is rebooting its operating system after a software upgrade. It makes me wonder about falling asleep — you know, that literal sensation of falling while drifting off. Am I falling into another dimension or reality when that happens? Whoa, dude.

During practice sessions I felt the sway myself and inflicted it on others. The falling-down drama is far more likely to occur in the seminars than elsewhere because there is such a strong morphic resonance going on with that large group of people. Not only is the synergism of the participants — both past and present — incredibly strong, but Bartlett and his team undoubtedly intend for certain conditions. This stuff may sound hopelessly namby-pamby to the uninitiated, but believe me, the man is *very* powerful. I certainly wouldn't mess with him. But don't get me wrong, he's far more inspiring than he is menacing.

It's definitely a bizarro experience, but most people who go to Matrix Energetics events have so much fun (and sometimes experience instantaneous healings) that they come back again and again. It's not cheap, and you could look at it as a money-making racket, but I say we're all free to choose, and the market determines the price, even when it's a unique monopoly service like this. One can always make use of library books and Interweb videos and embark on a homestyle quantum journey that's every bit as magical and satisfying without spending a dime. (Bonus: Bartlett's books are highly entertaining.)

⚡ ⚡ ⚡

After completing Levels 1 and 2, I tried doing some ME techniques with friends, though nothing eventful ever happened. But I wasn't really in the right frame of mind, and with this stuff mind is everything; it's all there is, really. Fortunately my personal funk didn't unduly color my perception of Bartlett and ME on the whole.

I had a private appointment with an established ME practitioner named Katrina who seemed pretty confident in her craft. I didn't give her any specific complaints, other than a general concern with my troubled love life. She performed her own version of Matrix

Energetics that was something of a cross between Janice's arm-waving clairvoyant energy work and a nimble belly dance, while she encouraged me to allow *my* body to move in whatever fashion it wanted to, unhindered by my mind. Soon I felt myself gyrating in a sort of infinity, or ocho, pattern. This continued for several minutes, subtly at first, then more pronounced. I had no idea what was going on—I wasn't consciously intending to move like that. And that's the thing about this matrix stuff. It's different, customized, and personalized every time, and so completely open to interpretation (or even interpretative dance) that there is no such thing as a typical session. What did it do for me, you ask? I have no idea. I can only say for sure that it was a strange and interesting experience.

At the end of our session, Katrina told me that the guy I was with at the time (Mike) did not really love me, and that once I broke free of him, a true suitable love—a beautiful amazing man—awaited, in about three months (why is it they always seemed to offer that timeframe?). This was comforting to hear, even if it was made of airy-faerie pixie dust. Well, to be fair, it was presumably plucked out of the infinite possible future realities from which I could choose. It just wasn't the wave I ended up surfing.

⚡ ⚡ ⚡

About a year later, I decided I was ready for another round of Cirque de Bartlett, so I registered for Level 3: the *Whizard's Training*. This time the curriculum had been culled from such diverse sources as ancient pagan magic rituals and modern pop culture media. There were so very many tools and techniques, it was almost overwhelming, especially because I hadn't really assimilated the ones I learned in Levels 1 and 2 yet. Modules and sigils and memes, oh my! But wait, I was just dwelling in the old academic mindset of sequential exhaustive learning, and there was really no need for that. It was just a toolbox, and even though there were all kinds of fancy specialized pliers and wrenches, I could just as easily get by with a favorite trusty hammer and screwdriver... which is more my style anyway.

When it came time to practice with the other attendees, some very interesting things transpired. I was in a much better mental state during this seminar and I'm sure that is what allowed it to happen. At one point when I played the practitioner role, a young Feldenkrais therapist was my "client." I employed one of the new tools we'd just learned, and did some freestyle stuff (which is heartily encouraged in ME), just unleashing my imagination and letting anything that showed up be okay, no matter how weird or irrelevant it seemed. She fell over and appeared to be having an ecstatic-revelation-while-writhing-on-the-floor experience. She was very moved, and told me as much. Her "issue" was something emotional so only she knows what effect the ME had on her, then or afterward, but it certainly *seemed* significant.

During another practice round, when I was the "client," another woman put the Matrix whamma jamma on me, and I fell over right away. (There were always people standing at the ready to catch you, by the way, so no one gets hurt.) I hadn't given her any "issues" to work on but was just feeling open to anything that might happen. To my surprise, she asked, "so what was up with your right ankle?" Well, I had injured it pretty badly a few months prior in a swing dancing freak accident, and it was still feeling kinda messed up but I had gotten so used to it that I'd honestly forgotten all about it. When I got up off the floor and walked around, the ankle was restored to normal—it felt completely, instantly healed! That was a nice bone from the universe, sanctifying my belief in quantum shifts.

The ankle healing illustrates the point that change occurs more readily when there's lowered resistance to it. Had I been actively thinking about my ankle and the "what is" condition of what was wrong with it, or badly wanting or needing it to be healed, it's less likely the healing would have taken place. It's even more important with really "big" topics where a lot of people contribute to a morphic field. As Bartlett says, you can't go head-to-head with cancer; there is just too much emotional energy behind it. It's been created as this big bad bogeyman. You can, however, play with imagery and see what it leads to. And possibly end up sending a tumor to another dimension. Or bringing the person into an alternate reality where the cancer doesn't exist. Yes, yes you can! If you really believe it. There is one

ME practitioner who, they say, specializes in just that: giving tumors a one-way ticket to another reality. Now there's a fresh take on medical tourism.

I know this stuff is really "out there" and incomprehensible to a lot of people. But that doesn't automatically make it fraudulent. Admittedly, it is difficult to experience firsthand such alternate realities, but we're typically too quick to conclude that they don't exist, or that those who proclaim they do exist are crazy. Richard Bartlett, for one, is not concerned that you'll think he's nuts. In fact, he will likely agree with you. He's not trying to convince anyone of anything, but is offering his knowledge to those who seek it. Really he's having a blast and inviting playmates into the sandbox. He's no benevolent dictator (though I suspect he's been the non-benevolent kind in another life...). It's power to the people all the way. He literally encourages people to invent ME tools of their own, saying, "hey, look, I'm just making this stuff up!"

To be honest, Bartlett's version of reality kind of scares me. He's been thrown across the room by powerful invisible forces and been taken on journeys that would make a bad acid trip look tame. If having those kinds of experiences is a precursor to harnessing one's superpowers, I might have to forfeit some of mine. Hopefully there is a happy medium for me. Maybe it's just that personality determines the nature and scale of the altered experiences, because his personality is most definitely large and in charge. Either way, the man is on to something. Something *big*.

9

MOVIN' TO THE COUNTRY
PART TWO

"Fix it with words
fix it with glue
fix it with money.
Simple."
♫ Laura Love

Summer was back in full swing, and there's nothing I like better than a good swimmin' hole on a hot sunny day. It just so happened, there was a most glorious one at the confluence of two cold clean rivers a mere six blocks from my new apartment. I was back in the saddle again, living the country dream life.

I had made my peace with Mike, and with the help of some good friends loaded all my earthly possessions into a Budget truck and headed north. There was something satisfying about having all my stuff together in one spot, because it had been scattered in multiple locations ever since I sold my house in Portland. It was a fresh start, in a new state and a new climatic region: the small but charming town of Twisp, Washington nestled in the Cascade mountains. I arrived late on a Saturday evening, just in time to sing a few karaoke tunes at the local watering hole.

I was infatuated. About five blocks long, the cute downtown strip held all the basics: a great natural food store, a bakery, a library, a brew pub, plus a few bonuses: a playhouse, an art gallery, yoga studios, and a semi-swanky Italian bistro. This was no ordinary redneck hole-in-the-wall; it was an exquisite outdoor playground for Seattle-ites and locals, and a hotbed of back-to-the-land passionate locavorism as well.

Williams, Oregon made Twisp look like a bustling metropolis —if Twisp was a one-horse town, then Williams must be a one-vole hamlet. Certainly Twisp had a different feel to it—much more light-filled, both literally due to the drier terrain, but also in a metaphoric sense, in terms of psychic energy and culture. The residents were mostly well-educated, and the economy was notably more diverse (most of it on the up and up, so to speak). Hugging the edges of town were rocky hillsides and striking views, particularly of the nearby North Cascades National Park, which remained delightfully snow-sprinkled through late spring. I was giddy with the sight of those mountains, and I got to see them every day. There was fresh air aplenty, and the rivers were about as pristine as they come in the lower forty-eight. There was peace and quiet most of the time. I say "most" because I lived right in town, in close proximity to other houses and small businesses. Had I lived a mile upstream and closer to the wilderness, I would have still been hearing chainsaws and other implements of man's dominion over the earth.   Such is the way of modern country life.

I lucked into a very sweet apartment in a hundred-year-old house, replete with gleaming wood floors, french doors, plate glass windows, cheap rent and wonderful landlords. The low overhead was a relief because even though I still had most of my life savings from the house sale, I would get worried from time to time about draining it. Thankfully, my friend Amy had done some legwork for me in securing the apartment, and I was "in like Flynn" during the peak rental season. Amy blazed the trail for me in more ways than one. She'd been living in that magical Methow Valley for a few years already, having migrated from Portland herself, happily forsaking the city life for epic hiking, skiing, and a robust local food supply.

Living right in town was ideal, since I was still carfree and because—I have to admit—I'm a little skittish about wilderness when it's just me and *it*, up close and personal. From the new digs I could easily walk or bike anywhere I needed to go, or else hitch a ride. It felt safe there because virtually everyone knew everyone else, and the valley is so isolated it seemed like there was nowhere to go... unless one was to long-haul it to a bigger town or to the city. Often when I hitchhiked, the person giving me a ride knew someone that I knew. One especially sweet woman picked me up, and before continuing on to our destination, nonchalantly took me along to visit her granddaughter for a few minutes as school was letting out. That's the kind of rural stuff that motivates me to live in the middle of nowhere.

One day I got a ride from a seventy-five-year-old man in a pickup truck who said he'd like to take me grouse hunting—ya know, to show a city girl the ropes—but couldn't on account of him being married. He had just left his doctor's office, and Doc had cautioned him to lay off the booze and cigarettes. He promptly lit a smoke, and after dropping me off was headed straight to the bar. Well, he looked pretty dang spry, so he must've been doing something right by enjoying himself in defiance of professional counsel. Perhaps that good clean country living is all it takes.   That's what I was banking on, anyway.

↯ ↯ ↯

In a town of a thousand people, the social scene was pretty limited. But that's exactly what I had in mind. There was little to distract me from my primary focus of Healing. I was determined to give that gaggle of cells-gone-wild a cease and de-cyst order—an eviction notice to move out of my ovary... and into another dimension. Or something.

I tried just about everything I knew of that was non-invasive. I began a detox cleanse and fasted for a little while, and took lots of herbs and supplements. I followed the alkaline-acid diet. And the blood type diet. I tried employing the theories and parasite zapping techniques that fringe-naturopath Dr. Hulda Clark raved about. I did affirmations and applied castor oil packs. I tried rapid eye therapy, hypnotherapy, EFT, TNT, NMT and some other alphabet soup that I've since forgotten. I probably would have planned a trip to Brazil to see John of God, had I known about him at the time.

I frequented the fantastic Twisp farmers' market and returned with a bounty of gorgeous local organic produce. I went through my cabinets on a witch hunt for toxics, eliminating plastic packaging of any sort because of its alleged talent in mimicking estrogen. I already had more than enough of my own, thank you very much. I scrutinized labels on shampoo or any other product I put on my body and ended up with very few options. Baking soda became my best friend. I even got inspired to exercise for a spell... though that sort of athletic vim and vigor doesn't ever seem to stick around for long.

I pored over various theories and advices via books or internet sites, especially anything hinting at the emotional origins of ovarian cysts. Those little Louise Hay books had been with me for ages, but I needed more than a one-liner now. I found a book entitled *Permanent Healing* by Daniel Condron that fleshed things out (ooh, bad pun) a bit more:

> *Ovaries*: difficulty in the use and power of the feminine expression, misuse of the receptive principle of creation.
>
> *Cyst*: unexpressed thoughts, resentment.

Huh. I didn't quite understand that "receptive power of creation" stuff at first blush, but it got the gears spinning. He also advised: "Practice meditation every day as a method of being receptive to the inner self. Develop an attitude of positive expectation in your daily life. Make sure you always have something to look forward to, to expect." Interesting, that word "expect"—like expecting a baby. It all made sense in some vague, circular-logic way but I wasn't very clear on what to do with it.

I was also calling upon energy healers of various kinds. It was handy that they usually work over the phone, since I was living in Nouveau Hooterville, but on my trips out of the valley, I would sample the goods whenever I could. Quantum Touch was one of the modalities, which seemed like your basic Reiki type healing, only turbo-charged with deliberate breathing patterns. I went to a weeklong Life Energy Healing School in Vermont, which covered an eclectic array of techniques and topics, but its main reward, other than the sheer pleasure of being in Vermont, was connecting with a new (or perhaps long lost) soul sister who was a fellow student. Sometimes life has us acting out these elaborate machinations just to get us in the same room with a certain person.

In one of the more potent energy healing tele-sessions, I was told that the trouble with my female reproductive system (or "the baby-making machine" as Lisa French would call it) was caused by a belief system—originating from my father and grandfather (and probably the whole dang clan)—that a woman's purpose is to have babies. Naturally, my conscious reaction to that sentiment was "fuck that misogynist noise!" I never wanted to breed and have never second-guessed myself (well, except for five minutes of madness that one time). But if everything was going on at the *conscious* level, I wouldn't be in this bind to begin with. The healer concluded that I had manifested conflict over my identity and purpose—and my very right to exist. Not exactly small potatoes. Surely that would qualify as unexpressed resentment, wouldn't it Mr. Condron?

Meditation was a fine idea. Initially, I set out to meditate every day, several times a day. This devolved into sporadic impulses once or twice a week. Was it undisciplined laziness or was I avoiding

101

something? I was still primarily seeking opinions and healing from sources outside myself.

⚡ ⚡ ⚡

One morning I awoke with the most bizarre sensations. My body was completely motionless and my mind was awake as I felt an incredible surge of energy. Not wanting to derail it, I didn't move at all for several minutes. I distinctly felt my *energetic body*—beyond my physical body—and it became about fifty feet tall while spiraling continuously. It was a wild ride. I asked myself pointedly "umm… should I be scared right now?" but decided to relax and go with it.

I don't know what that was all about or what triggered it, but nothing quite like that had ever happened to me. Well, actually, there were a couple other strange occurrences that same week. Like the morning I awoke and felt a man's arm around me, spooning me as I lay still (even though I was physically alone); it was vividly real and not the product of conscious fantasy. Or the afternoon when I sat down to meditate and felt my head being turned to the right, almost Linda Blair style. Who knows, maybe I received some sort of "activation" or something? I suppose at the very least, the point that there is much more beyond the "meatsuit" was well made—and well taken.

A few months later, when I reconvened with my favorite psychic tarot card reader Patti, she told me I'd been given the energetic equivalent of a swiss army knife and I was pulling out all the different tools and looking at them and trying to see what I could do with them. Wow, I liked the sound of that. I guess I knew about the corkscrew now, but what of the file or that fish eye thingy? What weirdnesses awaited me? I could only hope.

⚡ ⚡ ⚡

Another healing modality I took for a spin was called Reconnective Healing. I booked a long distance session with a practitioner in Texas. Interestingly, we weren't even talking on the phone during the healing. We arranged a time, and I laid down and relaxed as instructed, then she called me afterward to see how it went. This required a larger-than-usual leap of faith on my part, but a leap I was willing to make. I had nothing to lose, other than a cyst and seventy bucks.

I felt some tingling sensations while she sent me energy from the Lonestar state, but nothing extraordinary. I guess I was still a bit cynical. I'd experienced kinesthetic reactions to energy healing before, so maybe I was upping the ante now, requiring more pyrotechnics in order to be satisfied. Unfortunately, with subtle energies usually come subtle changes, and it can be hard to detect them when you're accustomed to coarser reality. What's more, it seems we don't get to consciously choose what the energy does and that's the frustrating part about energy healing in general.

A couple notable things popped in my mind during that session, seemingly out of the blue since they were unrelated to anything on my recent mental radar screen. One was an etheric other-worldly vision of romantic love—of me and that one man, whoever or wherever he is—which was a fun reverie at least (or perhaps a premonition, if I was feeling optimistic). It felt really, *really* good. If for no other reason, that scene and that feeling alone justified the expenditure.

The other extraneous thought was of my father. It was rare that he would ever cross my mind because we've never been close emotionally, and hadn't been close geographically for aeons. He was something of a hermit. So I was really surprised when the idea suddenly arose to ask him about his Navy days. He'd been in the service back in the '50s but I knew absolutely nothing about it, and it never occurred to me to ask him until now. This was novel. So after the session, I decided to do something extremely unusual: call my dad.

We had only talked on the telephone once before, several years back. I remember picking up the phone and wondering who it was on the other end, this man who obviously knew me. Once I realized it was my father, my mind started racing, wondering, "had someone died?" But no, his call was an unprecedented emotional response to something I had done.

I had found a little-known companion workbook to *The Celestine Prophecy* in the library and read it cover to cover. In it were exercises that got me thinking deep thoughts about my family, prodding me to examine the positive contributions each parent had made in my life and view their shortcomings with more grace and compassion. I was inspired; I'd never thought along those lines before. I made a custom artsy storybook birthday card for each family member —well, ever so slowly, over the course of a couple of years (and I might have lost interest before I got to all of my sisters, but such is the way of the temperamental artist). My father was the first recipient by sheer luck of the calendar. He was genuinely moved by it—I could hardly believe my ears. The mere act of openly expressing appreciation was so radical in our family that it succeeded in melting some seriously thick ice; *ice* being the operative word because Presbyterians are aptly known in certain circles as "the frozen chosen."

Looking back at my childhood, I had always been scared to death of the man. I never had the wherewithal to get to know him as a human being. But with time and distance comes the gift of a clearer and broader mindset. And ever since my parents had broken up for good, I was starting to see them more squarely as individuals, while ferreting out their individual contributions to the dysfunctional whole. It was one of my many fascinating self-appointed sociology projects.

At some point during my thirties, I started seeing how useful it had been to have a rough emotional start in life—it was all part of the path leading to where I was in the present moment. And thanks to the workbook, I could appreciate the parental traits I'd borrowed—like my dad's corny sense of humor, or my mom's take-no-prisoners hell-raising ways. Certain adages my parents were fond of reciting, such as "to each, his own" and "whatever floats your boat," sync up nicely with my worldview. But I often puzzled over the fact that, while she was saying those words, my mother always insisted there was just one right way (namely hers). Maybe those were my dad's mottos and she was just playing along but not really taking them to heart? Or perhaps she was teeming with internal conflict just like the rest of us humans.

The truth is that my father and I have a lot in common. This shocking realization hit me after I'd bought my first run-down fixer-upper house. A friend of mine who'd stopped by for an as-is tour asked me point blank, "are you completely *insane?*" Upon further questioning he learned that converting ramshackle buildings into cozy domiciles was something of a family tradition. I hadn't even connected those dots myself! Like my father, I had a driving, sometimes obsessive desire to transform things—some kind of subliminal preoccupation with alchemy—and a deep reverence for funky old antique objects. He had the wanderlust in his soul too, but it played out in the form of moving from house to house, because the life he'd found himself ensconced in—with a wife and four daughters to support—had effectively squelched any dreams of exciting adventure he may have been harboring.

More recently, another layer of the father-daughter enigma unfurled. I'd been working hard on my houses for years, doing all this macho stuff—sweating pipes, building walls, playing with power tools —doing things the hard way every chance I got. It was mostly fun, yes, and I learned a hell of a lot, but... *what exactly was I trying to prove, anyway?* I was taking do-it-yourself to an extreme level, working like a dog while other, saner friends were hiring contractors. True, I didn't really have the funds to farm everything out (which is why I now had the budget to live leisurely), but there might have been a happier medium. The revelatory answer was that I was trying to be like a boy —the boy who never showed up via my mother's womb— overachieving and unconsciously seeking the love and approval I never got from my father. Classic psychotherapy fodder.

ϟ ϟ ϟ

So I picked up the phone and called the guy. This time it was his turn to blank out for a few seconds and be surprised at who was on the other end of the line. After some brief niceties, I inquired about the time he spent long ago in the service of the U.S. Navy. It turns out he had been in Cuba just before the Bay of Pigs and had heard and seen some pretty intense stuff. And he'd been to Puerto Rico and thought it was simply paradise—and couldn't understand why so many

Puerto Ricans would want to leave.* It was incredible to be hearing these exciting personal accounts of international travel from a man who had grown up dirt poor in small-town rural upstate New York.

I decided to take a chance with the conversational momentum and tell him something real about my own life, not knowing how he might react. I'd learned to refrain from divulging anything personal to my mother or sisters, because nothing good ever came of that. But with my dad, there was no precedent. In a way, it was a blank slate and we were beginning a new relationship as adult acquaintances.

I told him I'd been getting into energy healing but took care to preface it with "well, I don't know if this is too weird for you..." to give him an easy out. To my great surprise he replied, "*well...* the supernatural is out there... if you're open to it." Holy crap! Was this really my father talking? I curbed my shock and seized the opportunity to inquire if he himself had had any experience with "the supernatural," as he'd put it. He got quiet for a minute then told me how, many years ago when his sister was pregnant, he suddenly *knew* that the baby was going to die. It wasn't a guess or a thought, but a sudden absolute knowing that came over him. It really freaked him out, and after a stillborn was delivered, he must have silently avowed to shut down his psychic capacities for good.

There was a stillness that followed. Probably no one had coaxed that story out of him in a very long time, if ever. He had never even told my mother in all their forty years of cohabitation. It was a rare moment of honest, real, vulnerable communication in the family. That seemed supernatural in and of itself.

⚡ ⚡ ⚡

My favorite energy healer, teacher and stand-up comic, Lisa French, was giving a talk on the mainland, so I arranged to attend it on one of my wandering adventures. If I didn't have these periodic trips to look forward to, I might have become bored and depressed living in

---

* Of course, the more politically astute do understand why, but this was a far more compassionate outlook than he formerly possessed. I was very pleased.

tiny Twisp. Of course, there were lots of potlucks and mildly interesting cultural events, but I was still hungering for cosmological know-how, magic and guidance at times. And, as usual, I needed a project, so trip planning would do nicely—no dust or fumes required.

Lisa delivered her dependable mix of comedy laced with undeniable truth; she was brilliant as ever. Among the attendees was a guy who must've arrived directly from 1987 via time machine: tight jeans, studded jean jacket, shades, long wild wavy hair. He had a British accent and I wondered why he evaded eye contact during the meet-n-greet sequence, because it was a small and otherwise openly friendly group. I had my answer during the introductions when a supermodel-like woman stepped up to the podium and introduced herself, pausing and adding elongated emphasis to her surname while looking in his direction. I instantly recognized the name as my mind flashed back to those heavy-metal-chick days in New Jersey long ago. Here was a bonafide aging rockstar with a clairvoyant trophy wife. Now *that's* rich, brother. It was an unlikely but highly amusing intersection of two very different phases of my life, proving once again that the universe has a fine sense of humor.*

Something Lisa said that day left a profound impression on my psyche. She was talking about karma, and how it's really not what we typically think it is—that all you have to do is forgive all parties involved, including yourself, and then poof! no more karma. But you have to *really* truly forgive and let go. You can't fake it. She had taught this to a young male student years ago who took it to heart. Steadfastly, he made amends in every facet of his life, then one day he joyfully jumped in the ocean and didn't come back up. She was a little weirded out at first (still feeling a bit responsible for others in those

---

* Sorry, I can't reveal the rock star's identity (wouldn't be prudent). The laughs didn't stop there. After the seminar I stopped in to a quickie-mart and the song on the radio was none other than said rock star's big hit from back in the day. Then a month later, when I called in for my free clairvoyant student reading (it was a perk from the seminar) it turned out to be a tele-class of two teachers and just one—you guessed it, rock star—student. When they got to my throat chakra and he was giving me vocal warm-up advice, I thought, "oh my god, it just doesn't get much better than this!"

days) but communications with him afterward indicated that he was extremely pleased with his choices and his experience that followed.

That really got me re-thinking my beliefs about suicide. Maybe it's not necessarily problematic across the board as an act, but it's the *emotional* component that often accompanies a successful suicide —or the erroneous idea that life will literally end—that is likely to cause a stumbling block in the so-called afterlife. It does seem feasible that someone could happily make a conscious choice to leave this physical plane and move on at any time, without negative repercussion. But I suppose "conscious" is the key word. Probably many elderly folks consciously choose to leave when they do; it's just more socially acceptable when you're old.

Because of the cyst-healing project, I'd been reading some of those annoying forgiveness books—you know, the ones that take up so much room in the self-help section of any metaphysical bookstore worth its salt. I began to adopt the radical perspective that all forgiveness is really of the self. The other people I previously thought I needed to forgive were just role playing. They're the hired guns, while I'm the one who wrote the play. Do I need to forgive the actors if I don't like the movie? (Well, maybe if it's Keanu Reeves doing Shakespeare...but otherwise, no.) When I step into my power, this all becomes ridiculously obvious. The logical thing to do is to thank the person for doing the job I essentially hired them to do. In other words, I want to be a benevolent reality-dictator and treat my employees well. And since I'm playing roles in *their* productions as well, I won't take it personally if they wanna get all agro or Steinbrenner on my ass. I can just shrug my shoulders, smile, and walk off the set.

ϟ ϟ ϟ

So I'd had a breakthrough with my father, but my mother was a tougher nut to crack. She remained something of a mystery. My last visit to her neck of the woods had been a total disaster—a classic example of that Ram Dass hilarity: "so, you think you're enlightened? Go spend a week with your family." I couldn't make it through a day, let alone a week. She was so incredibly dexterous when it came to

108

button-pushing; I was out of my league with the forgiveness stuff—at least when I was with her in person. They say that time heals all wounds, but distance can really do wonders.

I asked Patti for some insight: what was the deal with me and this woman? She told me a past life story in which I had done her a favor (*her* meaning my mother—only, she was just an acquaintance, like a co-worker, in that scenario). I had loaned her some money to bust out of an oppressive situation, and she wanted very much to repay me in that lifetime but never was able. So here she was in modern times, having cast herself in the role of mi madre, giving me sustenance during the crucial human-parasitic years, and planning to dole out an inheritance when she exits this mortal coil yet again. (Probably a humble inheritance by today's standards, though much more than whatever coins I'd tossed her in that other lifetime. Interest really accumulates over the centuries.) I wondered what yarns might be spun involving her and the other family members. Did she feel that she also owed them, or were they merely taking advantage of her generosity? Probably we've all been emotionally entangled for centuries on end.

Though she'd never describe herself as such, my mother is a sort of closeted pagan mystic—dabbling in astrology, numerology, tarot, Oprah. This stuff has been our main source of commonality, and probably why I chose her, among other reasons. We once visited a psychic together, and that was probably about the funnest activity we've ever shared. I don't know, but maybe, just maybe, on some level I was taking things further, extending a part of her life plan that got interrupted by childbearing? I've often wondered what she might have done, had she not been singularly focused on the lives of others.

Aside from that vaguely shared intellectual pursuit, we don't have very much in common. And in the absence of true emotional bonding, there isn't much authentic basis for a relationship beyond acquaintanceship. Which is fine, I finally realized. It was only problematic when I was trying to make it into something that it wasn't or couldn't be—usually in response to outside opinion of the way family *should* be. Look, I'm no ingrate; I'm just being practical. The solution I embraced was to simply accept everything as is, remain cordial but detached from the bio-family drama, and check in periodically. That allows me to think fondly of them just as I do of other casual friends. It's entirely possible to love and appreciate someone—such as a co-worker—without wanting to hang out with them, and that's perfectly okay.

⚡ ⚡ ⚡

On a subsequent travel adventure, I was sitting on an airplane and pulled out my new iPod. The prospect of having all my music at the ready, housed in one tiny appliance was very exciting. Come to think of it, I'd had no portable tunes since the days of the Discman. No wonder I'd been depressed. To me, music is a vital nutrient, and a deficiency is nothing short of insidious.

I plugged in the earbuds but was instantly annoyed to discover that the left channel wasn't working. I could find no settings to change the situation and I couldn't listen to it like that with the loud jet engine noise so I turned it off. I was upset because it was brand new and I was going to have the hassle of sending the thing back. But mostly I was pissed because I had no tunes right when I needed them to insulate me from further annoyance by my chatty seatmate. (It's funny how feeling annoyed leads to more annoyance, isn't it?)

It didn't take long to see how ridiculous I was choosing to be, and how it could not possibly be helping the situation. I recalled how they taught us, back in my Clairvoyant meditation classes, that we could apply energy and "ground" inanimate objects as well as live ones. Well, I had nothing to lose, so I calmed down, closed my eyes, and did some energy healing on the little gadget. After about five or maybe ten minutes, I opened my eyes and turned it back on. Lo and behold, both channels were working!

Now, I know you might be thinking what I was thinking at the time. Mere coincidence? I don't know, but I was very happy to have it be operational, however it happened. My mood was noticeably brighter, no doubt from that quick jaunt to Meditationville. "I really should do that more often," I thought.

Now, check this out. A few months later, I was playing the iPod at home and the same damn thing happened—only, the right channel was out this time. At first I was bummed, and figured it was defective and that it must have been a fluke that I'd "fixed" it on the plane that day. Then I thought, "well, if I did it before, I can do it again." But before I even started in with the energy work, the bigger message hit me like a C.O.D. (Conk on Dome—one of my dad's quirky sayings).

At some point, a few years ago, I had the fascinating realization that nearly every physical ailment I'd ever suffered had afflicted my left side. It was an eye opener, because according to Louise Hay and other new age mavens, the left side of the body represents feminine or yin energies and the right, masculine or yang. Well, just then, sitting on my couch with the iPod, I understood the symbolism in real time. The right side was "out" because I wasn't taking any assertive action at that point in my life—I was being too passive and I knew it. Just having the "aha" was all it took; I didn't even need to do any deliberate energy work. I turned it back on to find both channels working normally. That little contraption had done a fine job as messenger, its molecules at the beck and call of consciousness. And it hasn't misbehaved since. But if it does, I understand it to be a reflection of imbalance, of something in me that needs attention.

I'm well aware of how crazy this story might sound to the average person, but believe me, stranger things have been known to happen (especially at Matrix Energetics seminars). Some of my favorite and most well respected teachers have said that everything— and they do mean everything—is a reflection of the self. I find it more helpful to think that reality is interactive than assume that it's static. Helpful is helpful; and the proof is once again in the pudding.

If any "inanimate" object is going to play along with the human interaction game, an iPod is the perfect candidate because it's dedicated to me—no one else uses it. It's like my personal attitude adjustor. It's also fun to put the thing on shuffle and let it be a conduit for the perfect lyric-message in any given moment, like a modern electronic version of the I Ching. Try it at home, kids! Intention is a powerful plaything.

10

WHICH WAY TO AKASHA, PLEASE?

"Nice work if you can get it
and you can get it if you try."
♫ Ira Gershwin

Sometime back in the '80s I'd first heard about the Akashic Records,* a mysterious and wonderful "place," a sort of celestial filing cabinet in which, energetically, detailed information is stored for every moment in time—every thought, emotion, action and occurrence that ever was, is, or will be. Thinking about it gave me that excited tingly feeling—just like I used to get with the idea of seeing auras—because it just seemed so *magical*. I filed it somewhere between "just out of reach" and "just might happen." Why it cropped up again at this particular juncture is one of those marvels of serendipity. One day I found myself online, searching for and locating practitioners. Yes, there are people out there who will tune into your particular Akashic Records station—with your permission and your money of course— and get back to you with a synopsis of the broadcast. I think just about everyone has had some sort of paranormal experience, like psychic caller ID, or a premonitory dream, or those freaky "you owe me a beer!" say-it-at-the-same-time telepathy things. But to be able to access, at will, any particular piece of information from any timeframe for any person—well, that seemed like a superhuman ability reserved for the gifted and possibly socially alienated few. If they turned out to be authentic, I was more than happy to fork over the dough. And if not, it would be just another research expenditure to be rubber-stamped by my personal woo investigation bureau.

There was one such person in Spain who generated a long written report for me. I provided him with my name and birthdate via email; this was used to make sure he had the right person, and as far as I know, no astrological analysis entered the picture. The document contained all sorts of fascinating categories: soul group of origin; energy specialization in terms of chakras; soul specialization; Godspark (say, isn't that a Christian rock band?); life lessons; life mission, and more. He wrote that, while my "Godspark connection" was in perfect condition, I had no "spheres of protection" left, and he had gone ahead and restored those for me (sweet!... however it is that you do that). He elaborated on my "sixth chakra specialization" and it really did resonate with me—stuff about being direct in speaking my truth and

---

* Akasha is a Sanskrit word that supposedly means "aether," "space" or "sky."

114

struggling with the art of diplomacy, among other hot topics. I found it pretty ironic though, given that the sixth chakra is associated with third-eye seeing, because full-on proper clairvoyance seemed like something that was never going to happen for me.

I was taken aback by the description of my cosmic origin as a soul. Well, I wasn't quite as freaked out as I'd been when that Brennan healer implied I was an alien—but dubious nonetheless, especially because I was getting different stories from different sources. According to this Spaniard, I came from *Lyra* (not to be confused with Planet *Lycra*, which is an altogether different scene) about two-hundred-thousand years ago, and the Lyrans are a humanoid race that predate Earth's existence. He described the typical Lyran: a traveler seeking diversity, challenge and knowledge of a feeling rather than intellectual nature; easily uninterested and always willing to question anything that doesn't seem right; very nurturing, caring, affectionate. Sounds a lot like me. Then again, it sounds like a lot of people. But maybe that's just because I'm not the only Lyran in town? I had no way of verifying such tales, but I suppose it did feel good to read them.

A special message was conveyed from one of my guides: "Writers write. If you want to be a writer, then write." Busted! I hadn't been writing in a while, but noticed myself *talking* a lot about writing. With that kind of no-nonsense tough love, it sure sounded like a guide of mine should sound—straight outta cosmic New Jersey. Not knowing about my writing habit, he had couched the statement, saying it might be symbolic of something else, but I assured him that the dispatch was very appropriate and had no hidden meanings.

Other than that, there was a lot of generic-sounding content. Like self-love as a life goal. Isn't that true of everyone here? Maybe. Then again, maybe not. Maybe just a lot of us. Or maybe just a lot of the people I *happen* to meet. Regardless, it doesn't strike me as untrue. If fifty thousand people all go to the same stadium to enjoy a sporting event, do we question their individual motives for being there?

Overall, his report was good stuff and left me hankering for more. I found another Akashic reading service in England—a married couple, of which the man channeled and his wife acted as interviewer and secretary. This time I got an audio recording, and was able to submit particular questions to them beforehand. I found their answers pretty compelling because they went into accurate detail while giving me a fresh perspective about certain events in my past. The channeled entity who was purportedly accessing the Akashic Records on my behalf was a dead guy from a few centuries back. It was apparent that a lot of wisdom and love was coming through the transmission, and also a slight lack of hipness to modernity that made the character seem authentic. Smarts and love—that's what I look for in a disembodied helper. It's not a given, because dying doesn't automatically make you any smarter. But this guy seemed to pass muster.

They informed me of a "gatekeeper" (I know, very *Ghostbuster*-esque) who's been hanging around and working with me, unbeknownst to my conscious self. I suppose that's just another term for a spirit guide, but one with an extra-special key ring, who plays Gal Friday—updating and parlaying the Records to and fro. I liked the description of her, this lovely discarnate who allegedly had experienced only one human lifecycle. Anyone with the wherewithal to leave the bar after one poisonous round seemed plenty enough smart for me.

They also outlined a meditation routine that would be advantageous for me to adopt, with the goal of establishing greater connection and direct communication with my guides. It seemed like a reasonable plan. And although rigid routines typically don't stand a chance with me, I did take their ideas under advisement, subtly and sporadically incorporating them into my own version of sitting and tuning in.

Shortly after those readings, I heard about an Akashic Records workshop in southern California. How cool would it be to have a peek around those etheric archives myself? I imagined being handed a special golden key to the vault, then I'd run amuck in there, pulling out whatever records I fancied. For example, I would find out precisely what happened on that afternoon in 1972 when little Debbi got herself a concussion: what were the different parties thinking and experiencing in that moment? Or maybe I'd explore a glamorous lifetime in the 1920s as a flapper. Or go back—way back—to the beginning of it all and see what *that* was like. Or to the future…

I wondered how on earth this could be taught. Well, there was one way to find out.

⚡ ⚡ ⚡

The location of the workshop remained undisclosed until I forked over the money. I googled the address and plotted my mass transit adventure, arriving on the doorstep of someone's private home. That someone was a friend of the instructor, Emily, and another close friend of theirs was in attendance advertising her pet psychic services. When one of the resident cats rolled at my feet, this specialist informed me that the cat remembered me from another lifetime.*

The house was steeped in '80s décor and loaded up with every kind of new age or arcane tchotchke known to man. There were solid brass unicorns both large and small; a stained-glass ankh; a fountain water-feature; dolphins up the wazoo; loud wallpaper borders pasted high up on wedgwood blue sponge-painted walls behind clashing-patterned upholstery, purple curtains and two-tone brown sculptured carpeting; and a ginormous pyramid taking up most of one room, inside it crystal balls, Egyptian cats, a picture of some long-grey-haired dude named Braco (a sex symbol for new age ladies), still more dolphins, angels, feathers, pharaohs, candles, a crystal skull, chimes, stars, stones, whales, runes, and a bronze swan thrown in for good measure, all topped with a giant battery-operated Merkabah, spinning disco-ball style. I guess they were covering all the bases—just in case.

There were about a dozen people squeezed in, all of us women except for the Token New Age Male. During introductions he told us in a rather smug tone that he'd "always been on a *spiritual path*." Blech. (That reminded me of another class I took years ago in which The Token Male had stood up while proudly and dramatically proclaiming, "I've always been…. *mystical*.") I mostly found them to be unsmiling, humorless, and lacking in basic social manners. Hey, I'm no Emily Post but even I know you're not supposed to do things like double-dip

---

* Later on, throughout the workshop, she would frequently translate for us what the cats in the room were thinking. Oh, help me, Rhonda.

117

at the snack table with strangers.   There was one person I loved, though I barely interacted with her: a shy soft-spoken woman named Eva.   She was made of nothing but pure love and light, and she shined brightly in the room as she spoke of her pet cemetery work.*

Another woman, Karla, struck me as odd and awkward — almost borderline belligerent — but for some reason she took a shine to me and turned out to be very helpful.   She drove me to and from the train station, saving me a lot of time I would have spent riding the bus (which may or may not have been more interesting).   Karla was a serious one, very focused on community service, but also naive and childlike — not so much in the playful sense, but in a sad inner-child-needs-healing kind of way.   She gave me a CD of affirmations entitled *I Am Worthy!* It was a sweet gesture on her part, but being the brat that I am, I kept the thing under wraps to avoid any embarrassment of being seen with it until I was able to hand it off to the good people of Goodwill.   I wonder where it went from there.

The workshop content was a bit anti-climactic.   Emily managed to take a bigger-than-life magical concept and poke a hole in it, draining all the sparkles out and rendering it flaccid and mundane. Her technique was basically to get quiet and say a particular prayer. Apparently the precise wording of this prayer was the key to unlocking the Akashic Records, like uttering the secret word at the clubhouse door.   I tend to bristle when someone insists there is only one right way of doing things; it just seems plum unlikely.   I mean, are angel-amigos and ether-orchestrators really such sticklers for English?

Emily gave numerous examples of how her proprietary method could be put to use in everyday life: try going to the museum with "your records open," or watching TV with "your records open" and on and on.   It was "records this" and "records that," ad nauseam.   That prankster Mark Twain was laughing in my ear — something about hammers and nails.   She emphasized a big fear-based imperative to "close the records down" after these little jaunts.   I understand the value of being grounded — especially if you're going to drive or do

---

* Very Stephen King-ish, but she's making people feel better, herself included.

something practical or potentially dangerous—but she was warning us in such a grave tone that it seemed more than a little silly.

Emily kind of reminded me of Brenda, the wacky Theta Healing instructor in Utah. Emily had greater composure for the most part, though dysfunction was lurking just below the surface. She was more sad than anything, and fraught with health problems, and she used her position of authority in the spotlight to garner much-needed energy for herself (though in a much subtler, sneakier way than Brenda had done). Her life seemed tragic enough to warrant eyebrow raising. I couldn't help but wonder, if her self-proclaimed omnipotent tool really was alladat, why she hadn't effectively applied it to her own woes then. But there I go, being project-oriented again.

At the start of the workshop, Emily had told us to fill out a legalistic form and turn it in. It is, of course, commonplace for waivers to be required these days at just about any event thanks to our litigious society. But this one wasn't about not suing when you trip over the pyramid and scuff your knees. It was singly focused on the student agreeing to abstain from teaching the Akashic Record Prayer "in anyway [sic] with any person now or in the future." Well, I didn't like the sound of that secret society stuff and I thought it was dumb that she would need to so vigorously guard her less-than-spectacular spiel, especially since it wasn't even hers to begin with. I was feeling extra ornery—maybe because the garish décor was giving me a headache—and I just did not feel like playing a bit part in her control drama, if that's what was going on. So I didn't sign the paper.

To my surprise, she very slowly and painstakingly counted and reviewed the incoming forms while we waited idly, then addressed me directly, refusing to proceed until I scribbled my signature on one of the forms just as everyone else had. At that point, there wasn't much choice, since she had taken hostages. I could have refused to sign it and left, but I decided to play along, knowing the signature meant nothing anyway. (I'd reprint the special prayer here if it wasn't so damn boring.) I had traveled too far and was still way too curious about the Akashic Records to walk away on account of a minor tiff.

During the introductions that followed, she asked each of us to divulge some basic things about ourselves to the group, and to tell her specifically how she could best serve and teach us as individuals. When it was my turn, I answered in earnest, explaining that I am very much a free-thinker and that she would do well to not pressure me, but instead, allow me to arrive at my own conclusions in my own time. I said it, everyone heard it, and soon after she proceeded to do exactly the opposite. It's funny how people sometimes ask you questions when they really don't want to hear the answers. Well, probably she wanted to hear certain types of answers only.

I couldn't help but notice the gaping contradictions when they came rolling down the pike. Emily explained, "there are many ways to access the information—it's intention that matters." But an hour later, she refused to allow the wording of The Prayer to be altered as one of the women, Sherry, was requesting. Sherry, a feminist lesbian, found the biblical gender bias of "He" and "Him" to be cumbersome and distracting. Usually the students would nod in agreement with everything Emily said, so this was an unusual uprising. But Emily was not going to budge one iota, so Sherry accepted her lot and settled back into quiet submission for the remainder of the workshop.

Emily had us say The Prayer aloud together three times. It was going to take me a minute to warm up to that, if at all. Reciting things en masse, especially anything with a religious flavor, almost always gives me the creeps. But I silently read it to myself anyway.

Well, would you believe that in a room filled with a dozen voices, Emily singled me out for not chiming in? I suppose I was on her shit list ever since the paperwork incident. But I took it as a positive opportunity to sincerely remind her how to be a good teacher to me, thinking she'd see the light. Never mind that caca. Swiftly, she ushered me into another room and closed the door, then harangued me for disturbing the others by not saying The Prayer aloud. I found it hard to believe, since no one seemed disturbed (or disturbing) other than her. She actually offered to refund my money if I wanted to leave, but then... in her passive-aggressive manner backed off and assured me that it was *completely* up to me. I wanted to stay and hopefully have some direct Akashic experience of my own. I was genuinely interested in getting something out of this workshop, despite the current assaults on my sensibilities. So, stay it was.

Next was a journaling exercise that seemed like nothing much, initially. We went through our little routine of "going into the records" and then did some writing of a prescribed nature. From the list of topics provided, I chose to focus on obtaining meaning from an interesting dream I'd had that morning. I wrote furiously for a while, then pulled back and looked at my notebook, realizing that the stuff did not come from my usual conscious monkey brain. It definitely came from somewhere (or someone?) else. The meaning of the dream was pretty clear after that. Using "my records," in this case, helped me tune in to that greater mind or consciousness. But it wasn't an unfamiliar state; it was just the deliberateness of invoking it that was novel.

Even so, the results I obtained did not hinge on specific words utilized. I modified The Prayer to my own liking (we were saying it silently on our own by that point) and it had no deleterious effects. I'm convinced that intent truly is what matters, as words can have widespread variations in connotation. I think you've got to feel it and make it real for yourself, whatever that shapes up like, in order to propel the message out into the universe. All in all, there was nothing ground-shaking about her Akashic method. Probably I should have accepted the refund, but how could I have known that if I didn't see it through?

⚡ ⚡ ⚡

And so it was. Another episode in which I found myself playing the Heretic opposite the starring role of Lunatic. It's almost as if I'm just walking down the street of life, minding my own business and enforcing the sanctity and integrity of my own mind, when I periodically come across someone, like Emily, who seems threatened by this, so we end up in a tousle. Perhaps I'm doing them a favor by pushing their buttons, and they are helping me too—to learn greater self-love and confidence?   It seems to be working if that's the plan, because these experiences only strengthen my self-acceptance and resolve that I am, in fact, perfectly okay.   At least I'm walking away in amusement, not at all perturbed like I would have been in younger days. I call that progress.

11

THE RECONNECTION

"I'm standing in the yard,
where they tore down the garage to make room
for the torn-down garage."
♫ They Might Be Giants

Okay, so maybe I *was* getting a little bored. The snow sure is pretty up there in the Cascades, but you can only gaze out at it for so long. And I'm not big on skiing, or anything else that makes my toes freeze.

I'd gotten in the habit of listening to certain whack-job Interweb radio stations to pass the time and fill my mind with interesting new ideas. Many of the shows were quite thought-provoking, sometimes journeying to thoughts perhaps better left unprovoked—like virtual group experiences aboard spaceships. Others were touchy-feely broadcasts awash in angels and rainbows and sparkles and unicorns and meditations and love love, love love love. Ah well, you just have to be in the mood for such things.

One day I caught an interview with Dr. Eric Pearl. He was funny and irreverent, and I'm a sucker for that when it comes to the Woo. He was peddling a new brand of energy healing and—not unlike a package of organic convenience food—had a great story as to how it all came to be. He was the grand poobah of Reconnective Healing, the modality I had tried out recently with that Texan practitioner over the phone. I took the bait and ordered Pearl's book. It was a good read, and I felt no particular need to question the validity of his assertions or his struck-by-lightning storyline.

I would sit reading in my favorite glider chair, alternating between his book and several others on any given day. At some point, I started noticing a curious buzzing pulsating sensation in my hands and feet—not constantly, but often enough to command my attention, as I'd never experienced such a thing before. It wasn't painful or bothersome. It was just… there. In his book, *The Reconnection,* he talks about the possibility of being "activated" with this new energy just by reading about it. A similar idea was espoused in Richard Bartlett's *Matrix Energetics.* The premise is that ideas or practices have morphic fields that exist outside of our 3D reality, so there really are no barriers to accessing such energies, other than limiting beliefs that say it can't be done. But I didn't associate the sensations in my hands and feet with his curriculum until after the seminar—which I of course attended in short order to indulge my curiosity while keeping rural winter listlessness at bay. Their color glossy marketing materials were ablaze with glamorous head shots and pedestrian, hawkful statements such as: "This is NEW! This is DIFFERENT! This is REAL!"

During the two day workshop, I didn't forge any lifelong friendships, but I did meet a few fantastic human beings, one of whom I can still picture. She had the biggest warmest smile and she told me that when people ask her what she *does*, she simply responds "I play," explaining that it's important for others to know that this is indeed possible. Right on, sister. I loved that because I was always looking for more graceful ways to handle that inevitable rote icebreaking procedure strangers feel compelled to engage in. Sometimes I would conjure up a quick fill-in-the-blank answer: "Why, I'm a cosmonaut. And you?" I liked Tim Ferris' solution in his book *The Four-Hour Workweek*: he would casually tell them he was a drug dealer and that tended to shut down the interrogation process pretty efficiently. But I digress.

I met another interesting gal in the elevator and we became dining buddies for the weekend. We ate the yummy Seattle foodie food while swapping tales of woo-woo and man-woe. The other attendees were not all women, by the way. Perhaps sixty-forty this time? Therein lies the beauty of these cult-of-personality male energy healers—the ability to draw more from the ranks of their own gender. Apparently the testosterone content of the leadership allows the menfolk to feel more at home. Makes sense.

ϟ ϟ ϟ

The Reconnection staff stressed their definition of these "new *frequencies*": it was not just *energy*, but a combination of energy, light and information. This initially struck me as nonsense in the service of marketing because, after all, frequency is just one descriptive aspect of energy measurement, as is wavelength, and light is just another name for energy of a particular spectrum. Also, the idea that energy could be "new" didn't make a lot of sense to me. But maybe it's new to us here, at this point on Earth in the time-space continuum, coming from elsewhere, somehow? I was willing to curtail my skeptimistic ways and entertain the possibility that I was working with outmoded definitions. Perhaps there was something of merit going on, idiotic lingo notwithstanding.

The facilitators came around and "activated" our hands, and this I experienced kinesthetically as a cool breeze through my palms. That was notable since Reiki and other energy usually feels warm to me. There were lots of massage tables in the room, and when we started doing the hands-on work (finally, after what seemed like endless blathering) it was becoming obvious to me that this was, in fact, different from energy healing as I'd known it thus far. The "clients" exhibited visual signs of interaction with the energy... ahem, excuse me, *frequencies*. These signs, or "registers" as they are called, included rapid eye movement, involuntary muscle movement, and changes in breathing patterns. I could feel the energetic connection between my hands and the person's body, and it did become stronger with distance as they'd described—defying the normal expectations of physics. It felt kind of like pulling taffy. I could move my hands in certain patterns, or in certain locations, and notice the change in "registers." It was like playing a human theremin. What a fun playground! It was pretty exciting stuff. Here was some kind of tangible evidence, some real-time visible feedback that *something* was happening. But what?

The basic idea is this: we take in the energy, light, information, frequency, juju—whatever—then process and use it in the way that serves us best, which may be outside the grasp of the conscious mind (always a grey area). Healing may manifest on physical, emotional, spiritual, psychological, mental, or energetic levels, whether or not the recipient or anyone else perceives any change. As a facilitator of energy, waving my hands in the air like some sort of micro-supernal air traffic controller, I can hope or intend for the best but I don't get to consciously decide what happens. It calls for blind trust.

Unfortunately the workshop provided very few answers to satisfy my recalcitrant left-brain. It appeared to be aimed at the lowest common denominator in this come-one, come-all setting, as they repeatedly bludgeoned us over the head with a few simple ideas. The meat of it might have easily been covered within the confines of an hour, leaving much more time for the hands-on practice that was far more valuable and interesting—particularly when the rare individual was seen flopping like a fish on one of the massage tables.

Instead, we spent hours in tight rows of chairs while being admonished about the evils of other healing practices. Their point was that fear is counterproductive to healing, and when a person feels the need for crystals or talismans or some sort of outside power to help clear out or protect themselves and their clients from negative energy, they are bringing fear into the equation. Fair enough, I thought, but the fact that they dedicated so much airtime to this concern made me wonder what *they* were so afraid of. Ridiculing the foibles of ego-driven healers is a big part of Pearl's schtick—and he is pretty funny—but in doing so, he unveils his own egoic predilections, rendering himself just a little bit less endearing.

They also spent a surprisingly large chunk of time on the topic of private practice and charging money for healing services. I'd been toying with the idea of doing energy healing vocationally, though I wasn't ready to hang a shingle out. I was pretty uncomfortable with the idea of charging people a sizable fee for a nebulous service with a possibly undetectable outcome. I figured that people could just donate afterward if they were inspired. But the instructors were adamant about the need to set a standard price with no exceptions, no sliding scale, no donations. That sounded hardcore, and they did provide several reasons for their stance, but most of them left me unconvinced. For example, the fact that people routinely fork over boatloads of cash to conventional doctors with no guarantee of results. True, I thought, but those doctors went through more than a weekend of training (and have the student loans to show for it).

Regardless of such rationalizations, it comes down to the free market principle: people will pay for what they want at a price they are willing to pay for it. I was far more concerned with what my conscience, rather than what the market, would bear. One point they made was intriguing: a person who gets a bargain may expect, and only allow therefore, a limited result according to his or her perceived value of the service, so making it cheaper could possibly cause people to shoot themselves in the foot, so to speak, and resist healing. That seemed plausible in terms of human behavior (that's all economics is about really), though the probability is completely unknown, and possibly unknowable. It's all conjecture really. It seemed equally feasible to me that some individuals would be *less* resistant to healing when there is little or no money pressure in the picture.

Pearl's people attempted to infuse the curriculum with scientific proof. The head instructor had formerly worked as a career statistician. I know this because she managed to work that factoid into her monologue at least half a dozen times. I guess we were supposed to be wowed by her number-crunching street cred and inspired to swallow her offerings wholesale. But she hadn't blinded me with science; I was having the exact opposite reaction. From what little I'd learned in econometrics classes, statistics was a very crafty art form that calls for more, rather than less, scrutiny.

The charts were not unreasonable. Nor were they overly awe-inspiring. But I didn't need data to convince me that invisible energy exists, that spontaneous healings do take place, and that there are bonafide scientists on the task of documenting such things.[*] I'm not even particularly interested in the data. I just think that it's not a good idea to throw in the science card if it's not robust. There was a live demonstration with a random attendee who suffered from limited movement in her arms and shoulders. She was tested the first day in front of everyone, then re-tested the next day after some healing work had been done. There was a slight improvement, but this proved nothing because the small gain in mobility may have been readily achieved through stretching for all we know. It was an underwhelming display of prowess, permeated with cockiness. Perhaps Pearl himself does a better job than his protégés of pulling off these seminars, since he has an actual medical background. I could see why Richard Bartlett does not allow others to teach Matrix Energetics but insists on doing it himself. (Anyway, who could match his antics?)

The statistician's cohort, our assistant teacher, was an attorney. "If we can do this, anyone can" was the message they repeatedly imparted. Which was absolutely true. Heck, I was there doing it too. But what exactly were we doing? Their colorful career-change stories,

---

[*] Gary Schwartz and William Tiller, most notably.

designed to inspire, only fueled my cynicism. I mean, what's more lucrative — insurance and law or a shuck-n-jive dog and pony show? For some reason, these people really brought out the Doubting Thomas in me.

⚡ ⚡ ⚡

That seminar was Level One and Two, which covered the basic, or plain vanilla Reconnective Healing. Level Three involved learning how to do "The Reconnection," a specialized session during which they allegedly reconnect your body's energy meridians to the gridlines of the earth and beyond, and hook up your full twelve strands of DNA. Apparently having a dozen is our birthright, and not just the lame two strands we've been working with. This service is offered with the non-negotiable price tag of $333. They claim a certain vibrational affinity with the number three. (Are you snickering?)

Well, curiosity may have killed the cat, but the worst it could do to me was drain my wallet. I scheduled one of these two-part sessions with the assistant instructor from the seminar — yes, the attorney — who looked as much like a leprechaun as any human being ever has. The funny thing was that she was still actively working as an attorney, and had simply installed a massage table in one side of her law office to accommodate her new split career.

She arrived late for the appointment and unlocked her unheated office. I filled out some paperwork, then we chatted awkwardly while waiting for the space heater to do its job. She gave me a piercing look that really creeped me out, as if she were peering right into the very core of my being and sizing me up. And maybe she was doing just that — for good reason. My telepathic take on it was that she was trying to figure out if I was a troublemaker or if I was going to play along. I'll never forget the feeling — it was almost sinister. There I was, about to lay down on a table in a relaxed, altered state and trust this pernicious-looking leprechaun lawyer to wave her hands over my body and reconnect me to the earth's gridlines. Life is so surreal sometimes.

From my perspective there was no discernible difference between this Reconnection and the regular Reconnective Healing. Like so many other times, I did not feel, see, or otherwise sense anything in particular. Afterward I did a little research on the concept of connecting to the earth grid. Many people think that these gridlines do exist and that they are undergoing unprecedentedly high levels of flux these days. I wondered whether the Reconnection was equivalent to chakra-balancing—good for a little while, until everything shifts again (not nearly as long-lasting as balancing the tires on your car). Perhaps back when Pearl was first "activated," the gridlines were more stable and it made sense to do that? I'm just hypothesizing here. How can I really know about any of this stuff? The DNA topic is also very controversial, but at least lends itself to collecting tangible evidence, presumably. But without a lab and microscope, all I can do is wonder how differently would it or should it feel to have twelve DNA strands activated? I'm pretty sure I didn't leave with any new superpowers.

Part of Pearl's backstory was that his chiropractic patients had started spontaneously and involuntarily channeling messages to him, and there were six prominent statements that came up over and over again. (Ah, so maybe *that's* where he got the teach-by-bludgeoning idea?) Those statements were directed at him specifically and they made sense in the context of what was happening at the time, but when they were later parroted to us, some of them just seemed weird and inappropriate: "We are here to tell you to continue doing what you are doing" and "We have come because of your reputation." Huh?

I think the dude is genuinely gifted and inspired to help people, but his educational vehicle could use an overhaul. Maybe his woo-wares are just the tip of the energy healing iceberg, and there's more amazing stuff to be unveiled and brought to market. If that's the case, hopefully for his sake, he won't remain so attached to his schtick to preclude embracing the new goods. And for our sake, hopefully we won't need a middleman anyway.

After the seminar, I practiced on friends and other willing guinea pigs. Most of them described it as a positive, relaxing experience. Sometimes they would giggle, or feel like they were being tickled (they weren't—not by me anyway). That was fun. Some had visuals. Many reported kinesthetic sensations, sometimes in deferred areas of their bodies other than where I was "working." One of them told me her chronic pain was gone afterward—now, that's what I like to hear. I'm not sure whether her relief was lasting, but even if only temporary, it said something promising about the energy's potential... But which energy? Was it just my innate energy connection, which all of us possess to heal ourselves and others, regardless of the brand name that gets slapped on it? I do know that the seminar served to reignite my interest and bolster my confidence in playing energy-healer to friends, but who's to say that the same results would not have happened irrespective of my exposure to this "new" modality?

For a while, I considered signing up for Level Three so I could actually see what the heck they were doing with this whole gridline and DNA strand business (I imagined them drawing imaginary lines with their fingertips, and it's probably not much more exciting than that). But my attempts to register, or even have them execute the simple task of mailing my completion certificate from the first seminar, were thwarted at every turn. Ultimately, I took that as a sign; whenever things don't go smoothly, it means I'm on the wrong track. So I disconnected from their organization, satisfied to reconnect with myself instead.

12

ADVENTURES IN CONSCIOUSNESS

"Deep in my heart,
the answer, it was in me."
♫ Lauryn Hill

"I am more than my physical body..." began Bob Monroe's time-honored affirmation. This I recited silently, lying in bed in the comfort and quietude of my Controlled Holistic Environment Chamber, otherwise known as a CHEC unit, before embarking to realms unknown. With hemi-sync frequencies playing in my ears through high-end stereo headphones, I could actually "see" patterns of colorful concentric vibrations inside my brain—just like the depictions in the literature! What's more, I could see them just as well with my eyelids open in the pitch dark and no visual stimuli to distract me. At last, it seemed the lens cover had been removed from my third eye.

⚡ ⚡ ⚡

I'd discovered The Monroe Institute (TMI) in typical metaphysical nerd chain-smoking fashion: by reading about it in a book that came recommended by another book. On TMI's website I found descriptions of all sorts of intriguing programs with clever familial nomenclature: Guidelines, Lifelines*, Heartline, Starlines, Timelines. Mostly I was drooling over the one that flaunted spoon-bending, because to me telekinesis was about the coolest thing ever. Still, I hemmed and hawed about the expense of it, because I would need to take a prerequisite first—the Gateway Voyage—and these were week-long residential programs that included lodging and meals.

Hemi-sync. Sounds like something under the hood of a muscle car, doesn't it? It's short for hemispheric synchronization. We humans are only capable of hearing one frequency at a time apparently (simpletons that we are), so when you put different frequencies in each ear, the brain splits the difference and creates a single, unified vibration. Say it's 100 Hz in the left ear and 105 Hz in the right: the brain creates a 5 Hz (theta, in this case) wave across both hemispheres.

When the two halves of your noggin cooperate, amazing things are known to happen: altered states, increased focus, turbo-charged

---

* In this program, participants "travel" to other "locales" and help guide lost souls "homeward." Sounds to me like the ultimate in social work.

meditation, visions and epiphanies—stuff like that. Many people have out-of-body experiences (OBEs). In fact, that's how it all began for Bob Monroe. Back in the 1950s, he spontaneously launched into his "second" or energetic body, and it scared the bejeezus out of him. Being a fairly conservative fellow, he was quite distraught for a while, finding almost no information or personal support in mainstream medicine or science, but eventually learned to accept his lot and relax, then began conducting his own exploratory research. Years later he founded the Institute and became that needed information source for others, continuing his research activities on a shoestring budget and eventually offering structured open-to-the-public programs for the purpose of self-exploration. And along the way, he wrote some pretty riveting books about his fantastical out-of-body adventures.

Volunteer studies and data gathering resulted organically in the identification of certain distinct levels of consciousness, and an utterly fascinating cosmology was unveiled that was free of dogma or ulterior motives. Normally we think there are far fewer options: ordinary waking consciousness, sleep, unconsciousness such as in a coma state, and perhaps the subconscious as accessed during hypnosis. Yet, there is more, so much more. Monroe, with his sound engineering background, cooked up special recipes of frequencies optimized for reaching each of the specific states of consciousness or "focus levels." A handful of theta, and dab of gamma, a pinch of beta, a lizard's gizzard...

ϟ ϟ ϟ

Curiosity won out over frugality, and I found myself there in Virginia, excited to blast off on my Gateway Voyage. I guess I got a little crazy because I also registered for their special New Year's Eve program a month later. Being single, I never quite knew what to do with the holidays, and exploring alternate modes of consciousness was a lot more appealing than holing up in a ski cabin with six couples and a bottle of something-or-other.

The Institute sits on a sweet rural piece of hilltop real estate with sweeping views of the Blue Ridge Mountains—a lovely setting for meditation. During program breaks we'd take walks and reground our bodies in the Appalachian splendor. It's tucked away about a half hour from Charlottesville—a rather curious oasis, ideologically speaking. I was surprised to find that many locals had never even heard of TMI. In the early years, Bob had kept things tightly under wraps for fear of being ostracized by his business community. For me, that factoid came as a potent reminder of just how much times have changed. It seems today, at least on the west coast, that nary a yoga-going businessman would bat an eye at the mention of OBE.

Inside the homey '70s building were the CHEC units, common areas for meetings, and a cozy dining room. The staff was very attentive in the way that only Southern hospitality can provide. The only thing they couldn't remedy was the insect invasion, which was plaguing not just the Institute, but the entire region. The buildings were overrun with ladybugs and stinkbugs—the latter looking like some sort of hybridized miniature WWI army tanks on legs (they fly too... eek). Rumor had it that an overabundant ladybug population prompted some brilliant government employee to import the stinkbugs as a predatory solution. But the stinkbugs had fallen down on the job —perhaps thinking the ladybugs too cute to catch and eat, or else the girly critters were just too wily and wiggly to be caught—and now there was a glut of both*. I kind of got used to seeing them around, even though they gave me the heeby-jeebies. As long as they stayed out of my CHEC unit, things would be hunky-dory.

The trainers, John Kortum and Penny Holmes, had comedic chemistry of a rare and glorious potency, and I felt I'd gotten my money's worth from just one day of the John and Penny show alone. Any existential epiphanies headed my way would be mere gravy.

Penny, who looked and sounded a lot like Lauren Bacall, was the late Bob Monroe's stepdaughter, though she hadn't climbed aboard the family enterprise until a bit later in her life. With charismatic wit

---

* When I returned to the Institute a year later, the ladybugs were mostly gone but the stinkbugs sure weren't. So maybe the little predators had finally stepped up. But still, it left the humans with an awkward situation. Ah, the human micro-management of the eco-system—more mystifying than a journey to the land of lost souls.

and deadpan delivery, she shared personal anecdotes with us: her mother had been eccentric alright, but life got even weirder when she met and married Bob. I loved her curmudgeonly humor. With the slightest smirk, she would nonchalantly slip in neologisms like "churchianity" or the "newage" (rhymes with sewage) movement," and urge us not to blindly accept any dogma that Bob or the Institute might be peddling. I especially loved that part—the forthrightness and unquestionable respect for individual sovereignty that TMI fostered.

John was equally lovable. He'd come out with some profound statements such as, "a turbulent childhood is a spiritual advantage." Apparently he's got special psychic superpowers and a side-circus of his own, but his self-promotional activities were tastefully minimal.

The attendees totaled twenty, with equal gender representation and far more diversity than I would have imagined, ranging in age from the late thirties to one particularly childlike 83-year-old Alaskan woman. Certain uproarious personalities (most notably a certain wonderfully riotous gay minister from California) combined to create synergistic fun the likes of which that place may have never seen before or since. It was an eclectic but happy family. There was a macho smoker from Mexico, a cute young German gal, a very happily married couple exploring side by side together, and an assortment of other characters. I got a kick out of hearing an engineer from New Jersey and a former-cop-turned-military-contractor talking about auras and energy fields.

Our days began around 7:00 am—I'm guessing, because we were encouraged to forsake our timepieces and loosen our connection to time in general (but it was decidedly uncreepy compared to that Vipassana retreat). During the night, a special hemi-sync "Super Sleep" recording played low in the background on a 90-minute loop corresponding to natural sleep cycles. In the morning, the volume was raised and a posthumous Bob Monroe recited affirmations in my ears. This was followed by *Cable Car*, a spunky, quirky original musical composition of his that repulsed some people, but I absolutely loved it. The more eccentric Bob seemed to get, the more endearing he became to me. I could picture him, plunking away happily on that Moog organ, his latest toy. He was the grandpa of my dreams. And in that way, not so unlike my actual grandfather who would sometimes sit upstairs in his 1940s-built home playing a cheesy little Sears organ while gleefully crooning *Beautiful Dreamer*. Good stuff.

There was yoga before breakfast, led by the sister-in-law of the founder's stepdaughter. (Well, nepotism isn't necessarily a problem... unless it is. And it wasn't.) The trainers emphasized the need for physical exercise in order to stay grounded. It helped me to keep from falling asleep during the hemi-sync exercises, which was a problem in the first day or two due to jet lag. I was told it didn't matter if I fell asleep because I was still taking it all in, despite my lack of conscious participation. But I was paying a lot of dough and really wanted to be present and remember it all. (In subsequent programs, I would plan to arrive a few days early to get in sync with the time zone.) We did about four or five hemi-sync exercises each day, meeting together briefly for an explanation, then retreating to our individual CHEC units "by way of the bathroom"—because no one wants to have an out-of-bladder experience. There was excitement in the air during these comings and goings because, increasingly, we relished the novelty of each exercise and each one's potential for mind-blowing adventures or personal epiphanies. It was definitely a well-crafted program.

The exercises were designed to gradually introduce us to various "focus levels." Each recording began with soothing ocean sounds and a guided narrative explaining the fourfold preparatory process, the first part of which was the creation—in our thoughts or minds' eyes—of a big heavy box with a lid: the Energy Conversion Box. In it, we'd place anything meddlesome—worries, doubts, fears, expectations, emotions, random thoughts, distractions, mental chatter, etc. There were jokes about putting one's mother-in-law in there, which cued Penny to recount this fun tale from another Gateway session: a very attractive woman found herself confined in a dark box during an exercise, and later learned that several of the men had put "her" in the box because they were feeling a bit... um, *distracted*.

Next was the resonant tuning, which sounded more like dissonant toning to me. The first time through, we did it as a group in a circle—oh no, the kumbaya shit! And just when I'd put my faith in John and Penny. Fortunately, after that one digression, toning was

138

done in the privacy of our CHEC units with headphones (and they were good ones because I didn't hear my roommate and assumed she wasn't able to hear me either, thank god). I gave it a try and was genuinely surprised when a strong tingling sensation started up one side of my body. With that personal confirmation, I conceded the importance of resonant tuning, however musically objectionable it was. (I suppose fifty million ancient Easterners can't be wrong.) I also noticed that, oddly, the sound seemed to originate from and percolate in only one side of my head, which kind of freaked me out momentarily until I decided to try consciously willing it to jump sides, or occupy both at once — which actually worked. What was that all about?

The third prep step was the creation of a resonant energy balloon or ReBall. It's similar to defining one's auric boundary, yet more dynamic. I had the sense of becoming a human Tesla coil. The ReBall serves to define and protect, but also to magnetically draw to oneself the energies intended for any particular exercise or purpose. Penny likened it to an airbag originating in the toroidal field of the heart.

The final step, before launching into god-knows-where, was intention-setting in rote form. Bob Monroe's affirmation was the only thing even remotely close to dogma that we needed to play along with:

"I am more than my physical body.
Because I am more than my physical body I can perceive
that which is greater than the physical world. Therefore, I deeply desire
to Expand, to Experience; to Know, to Understand; to Control, to Use such
greater energies and energy systems as may be beneficial and constructive
to me and to those who follow me. Also, I deeply desire the help and cooperation,
the assistance, the understanding of those individuals whose wisdom,
development, and experience are equal to or greater than my own.
I ask for their guidance and protection from any influence or any source
that might provide me with less than my stated desires."

I had no problem with these words. (Memorizing them, however, was another story. As you can see, verbosity is a trait that Bob and I share.) It pays to be precise in your mental communications

139

—with whomever it is you think you're communicating. But it's also perfectly acceptable and recommendable to convert words into a succinct mental concept, or even a symbol. There's plenty of room for customization.

Our first stop on the Voyage was Focus Level 10: "Body asleep, mind awake." It was similar to meditative states I'd experienced before, but it was a much deeper kind of relaxation, thanks to the prep and the hemi-sync technology. Even my mental chatter slowed and quieted down somewhat. Progress already.

Next was Focus 12: the "State of Expanded Awareness," of nonverbal communications, the Gestalt, sensations, inner resources, guidance and humor. (Yay for humor. It's no wonder this became my favorite focus level.) I was amazed at just how different Focus 12 felt from 10. I immediately saw lots of stars… was my consciousness out in space? There was floaty movement. Mind you, my physical body was completely still, as I'd just passed through Focus 10 to get there, so this movement was of my *energy* body. What a trip. I'd had some previous sense of it, but those were much milder experiences, and they just happened to me at random. This was something else—an experience you could consciously control, and then experiment and play. One exercise in Focus 12 had us doing free form movement, like log-rolling. It was mind-blowing actually. Though I can't say I went hog-wild because I felt a little restrained. It made me wonder if this was related to my queasiness on rollercoasters, and whether this new tool could help me overcome stuff like that. And I had a fun little "aha!" moment when I recalled the idea of thought-propulsion spacecraft. With my energy body "vehicle," thought was the *only* way to effect movement.

Vibrationally, Focus 12 seemed like a fine launching place for an out-of-body experience. I was told that you just need to relax into that cataleptic state and increase your vibration to a certain level, and that there are certain tricks to employ. I didn't have a classic OBE where you actually rise up and view your physical body below, but then again it wasn't something I aspired to at the time. Perhaps I was carrying some buried fears preventing it? Regardless, I'm fairly sure

"I" (or part of me) was outside my physical body, and at the same time there was a tingly-all-over sense of expansiveness.

At some point I "clicked out," as they say—not sleeping, yet with no conscious recollection of where I was, how much time had elapsed, or what had occurred. A possible explanation for "clicking out" is that when the conscious mind would otherwise interfere, it gets left out, like a younger sibling trying to tag along on a date. Another theory is the so-called Magellan Effect. It's that old story of how the Native people could not see the big European ships out in the water because they held no concept of them—they'd never seen or heard of such a thing. So in this case, my conscious mind may have been blanking out because it just did not know what to do with this new vibration or whatever I was experiencing—it simply didn't recognize it.

Eventually each exercise gently returned us to C1, the normal waking mode of consciousness. Apparently it's not uncommon for people to be spaced out and not fully return—not in some super scary mind-lost-to-the-zombies way, but because they're so blissed out they don't want to get back to so-called "real life." There were hilarious signs in the bathrooms that pleaded, "Make sure the shower curtain is inside the shower. 1! 1! 1!" (Yeah, we're talking to YOU, space-cadet).

Halfway through the program, we were introduced to focus level 15: "where Time Does Not Exist," also aptly described by one participant as the "teflon place" where emotions do not stick. The Field of All Possibilities, the zero point field. Blackness. Void. Nothing. All things. No time. All time. The trainers told us two monks had come to TMI and were amazed to be brought to this "place" in just one morning that had taken them fifteen years of meditation to reach. "American innovation!" they exclaimed. Or so the story goes.

To me, Level 15 was exceedingly calm, velvet black, and yes, seemingly outside the realm of time. Which, come to think of it, is not an everyday feeling. I think most people have experienced weirdnesses with regard to time—time warps, the extreme slowing or quickening of time, but rarely the total absence of it. They say Focus 15 is especially good for obtaining creative ideas and accessing past and future events from the endless possibilities that exist. Conceptually, it is the crucible in which time rests. Whoa, dude.

My initial reaction to 15, however, was "boring!" That is, until Penny explained that I needed to initiate things, make things happen for myself, whereas in Focus 12, the joint was jumpin' and I was just checking it all out, responding to it. Of course, taking initiative was always an option in any Focus Level, but there was a great deal of stimuli in 12 by default, so it was easy to "surf" with no particular purpose (kind of like living in Santa Cruz). Focus 15 is more of a blank slate. We did a "free flow" in 15 that was referred to as a "soul spa." For this exercise, the big paper on the conference room easel said "Relax. Have a good..... *time*?" Clever.

In free flow exercises, I would silently ask questions and receive answers in pictorial format, sometimes in blurry, cryptic imagery and other times things were very clear and symbolic in an obvious way. It was similar to dreaming but with greater awareness. Often I'd get a direct mental download, a succinct instantaneous knowing that accompanied the visuals and made interpretation very easy. It was fantastic to take it all in while remaining fully conscious, as too often the dream state is a half-forgotten hazy memory.

Many exercises had a specific theme or purpose. There was one making use of "dolphin energy healing" through imagining or allowing dolphins to show up. During that one, I felt an energetic surge and "saw" dark areas of my body lighten up in the blue emotional body map we were instructed to visualize. Interesting... but relatively subtle, because other people reported amazing spontaneous healings. But then, it never pays to compare oneself to others.

During the set-up for a Focus 12 exercise called "Vibe Flow and Beyond," an older note-taking woman asked innocently "now why do I want to increase my vibration?" Penny replied with characteristic dry humor, "because the current vibration in the world sucks."

ϟ ϟ ϟ

There was only one person in the group who I found annoying. Those are pretty good odds, really—a mere five percent—especially considering my track record. Well, someone had to be the resident narcissist, and Naomi was it. During the group debriefing sessions she offered longwinded dramatic accounts of her personal experiences in each and every exercise, as if it were the most titillating thing on the planet (well obviously it was... for her). If everyone had followed suit, there would've been no time left for the actual program. I was starting to feel like I knew more about Naomi's experience than my own. Then Penny announced one morning, "if you're feeling that reptilian energy right about now—that cranky feeling, wanting to be left alone...maybe today you've decided that so-and-so is a jerk—well, you're right on schedule." Hah! Validation is a many-splendored thing.

Besides hemi-sync exercises, they threw a few other goodies into the mix. One evening, a surprise guest gave a talk. It turned out to be Joe McMoneagle, first and foremost Remote Viewer formerly employed by the U.S. government, and author of *Memoirs of a Psychic Spy.* The back story of the Stargate project and other tales from Joe's life were enthralling to say the least; we were hanging on his every word, reluctant to even take a restroom break for fear of missing out. (Oh, wait, I guess I do still have some fear.)

On another day, the trainers played for us a conversation recorded in the '80s between Bob Monroe and an institute research volunteer who was in some sort of altered state. Rather unexpectedly, she began channeling an outside entity. Her voice changed to that of a young Scottish man in the 18th century who had apparently died but didn't know it. He was extremely confused and scared. We listened in amazement as Bob calmly talked the lad into letting go of that dreaded, infinitely-repeating reality he was trapped in to "go to the light" by getting him to look up and notice other souls (his parents) and ecstatically move toward them. It was very moving to be privy to this kind of soul rescue work, and there was no reason to believe any aspect of it was fabricated. To me, there is no question that life goes on

---

* I know that some people are freaked out by TMI's connection to this variety of questionable government activity, and that's understandable, but remote viewing is just a tool (and a really cool tool at that). The fear of evil is, well... *fear*, and personally, I'm not really into fear.

after physical demise. But what sort of life? This is where Monroe's explorations and cosmological formulations get very, very interesting.

In our group discussion that followed, someone asked why people such as ourselves, in physical living human form, should be the ones rescuing lost souls. Are there angels somewhere who are slacking off? The answer has to do with vibration. Those souls "stuck" in their earthbound realities—because they simply cannot conceive of or believe in anything else—are closest to us in vibration. So it's sort of like using a peer to talk to a kid who won't listen to adults. And for those lost souls, it is the *emotional* level of vibration that locks them into their realistic earth-like realities. Life systems, according to Monroe, incorporate dozens of levels of consciousness, from plants and animals, to humans, to various non-physical beings. After physical "death," we stop first at Focus 23 (also known humorously as Club Dead) and may end up lingering in the "belief system territories" possibly indefinitely (but then, time is not perceived there as it is in this realm). Focus 27 is "home"—that's where you want to hang your non-physical hat, ultimately, and you can make it into whatever you want it to be with the power of thought. The numbering of the focus levels seems to imply a hierarchy of some sort, but that's not the case or the intention; it's just a convenient labeling system.

Naturally, for the rest of us, it's all speculative, and Bob himself was big on self-exploration as the only method of knowing. The important point is that, regardless of the analytical constructs, there are obvious lessons we can extract for our here-and-now existence. How often do we get locked in to our thought-forms while incarnate? It really is the emotional component that keeps us imprisoned. I don't know about you, but I'm all about busting out of the clinker.

They showed a great classic short film, *Powers of Ten*, and a full length movie one night—which I skipped, happy to have some unscheduled alone time. The morning of silence was lovely, as was much of the music John and Penny played. On a few occasions they read poems over the P.A. and I suspect my heart was wide open because the Rumi selection *What Was Said to the Rose* nearly brought me to my knees. It's not uncommon for people to have emotional

144

breakthroughs at TMI, as there's no telling where the Gateway Voyage might transport a person.

So very many messages came to me over the course of those six days. Each little piece, every silent question and answer, vision and "download" was meaningful. But absolutely personal, so I rarely shared the details of my process publicly. When I was undergoing some intense emotional processing one day, I kept it to myself, though I suppose it was obvious from an outside perspective. It actually catalyzed a wonderful new friendship, because one blue-eyed beautiful soul of a man was inspired to offer me solace and hugs, enabling true connection between us (and we've kept in touch ever since).

Occasionally someone would receive a specific message for another person in the group. I had a few experiences like that, on both the receiving and transmitting end. Why? I have no clue. Just another mystery to ponder. I suppose that people often deliver messages to each other in everyday life, but in a more covert fashion.

The final vibrational stop of the Voyage was Focus 21: "The Bridge" to other energy systems. The concept was spellbinding. What exactly are those *other* energy systems? Aliens?!? How can I tap into them? Is that how healing miracles are accessed? I want in! Let me in!! (*Where's that confounded bridge?*) Well, as it turns out, Gateway takes you to 21 and no further. And further, my friend, is where you need to go in order to cross that bridge. It's that old free heroin gag again. But Focus 21 was pretty exciting on its own, I must admit.

The journey from 15 to 21 was a colorful one—literally so, because each focus level en route had a color associated with it, and I experienced this as the act of passing through a series of connected rooms, each filled with a different vibrantly colored light. Focus 18 was my absolute favorite. Rose pink, it's the place of unconditional love. What's not to like about that? I got lost in there for awhile, like the kid in Willy Wonka's Chocolate Factory who wanders off the tour, lured by the everlasting gobstoppers.

Focus 21 itself was white and bright. It reminded me of the "seventh plane" in Theta Healing, and for all I know, they are one and the same. Initially, I emerged into a grand ballroom, all white and sparkly-spangly, elaborately appointed, very lush and inviting. (No wait, actually that was my second visit to 21. The first time was reminiscent of a bad but mercifully brief acid trip, filled with melting faces, string theory and other inexplicables... I'd almost forgotten about it because it was so unsettling. Imagine my relief when the set changed the second time around.)

It felt like this etheric ballroom I'd entered was a sort of welcome area for me to launch into 21, and that is where I met with angelic-looking entities—spirit guides? or parts of myself, or both, I do not know—who took me on a fantastic journey, loosely based upon my questions about energy healing. Some of what I got is difficult to articulate. It felt like I was being taken over tremendous distances at incredible speed and information was communicated via demonstration and telepathy. Perhaps I did cross some bridge and go into other levels beyond 21. It was a remarkable experience—very real, vivid, and interactive—and I came away feeling profoundly moved and satisfied with myself and my life in a whole new way.

At some point I was shown how my negativity and judgment had been getting in the way of love and happiness and healing. In the middle of a seemingly unrelated scene, a cute little girl about two years of age strolled in. I asked what her name was and she said "Naomi." Uh-huh, I get it.

One of the last exercises had us open up that Energy Conversion Box we'd been stashing our fears and mental distractions in many times a day. That was a hoot. I lifted the lid and removed the contents one by one, flinging them as far and hard as I could, while a hilariously whimsical stereophonic sound effect played in my headphones. It was a joyous act of emotional release. My "stuff" appeared in the form of a toy plastic dinosaur, then a huge heavy firehouse, and also a large gift box with a pink bow. With that last one, I just had to peek inside before chucking it. It was a monkey! Very funny. I understood instantly that this represented my monkey-brain mental chatter. Spirit guides have a great sense of humor sometimes.

Our final night together included a super-fun raging dance party with old-school booty-shakin' tunes, thanks to John Kortum. Lightening up and letting loose was just what the doctor ordered... Dr. Disco that is. It already felt like New Year's Eve.

꙳ ꙳ ꙳

A few weeks later I was back at TMI, all twitterpated about the NYE program and the possibilities it held. I was still high on Gateway, so to speak, and presumed I was in for more of the same. But these resident programs can be so strange: you're thrown together in close proximity with a group of strangers, some of whom have you convinced that your only commonality is awkwardness. But before long you get so used to being around them that they seem like family, and when it's all over you feel kind of lost without them. All this inside of a week's time.

It took me a little longer to warm up to the new group, which was decidedly older, more sedate, and fewer in number. Even the trainers were a letdown *initially*, because the John and Penny show is a tough act to follow. I'd heard that there was nothing quite like a Gateway experience, and now I understood why. With the newbies, there's a certain openness to the unknown that's accompanied by a willingness, or even a need, for social bonding. But with the graduate programs, they say people tend to be more self-directed and self-contained.

The curriculum was cobbled from a variety of sources, with over-arching themes of reflecting, learning, and intending. I'm sure this was a fun creative gig for the trainers, Carol and Karen, because of the artistic license afforded them. Now, let me tell you, these were two ecstatic chicks. That's what I like to see in my leadership! Some aspects of the program were New Agey and a little sappy, but I suppose that comes with the territory of blissed out people in this line of work.

Among the attendees was a European couple who were fond of dark techno music, and they shared my distaste for the synthesizer-dominated Metamusic that was sprinkled liberally throughout the program. If anything though, I was as amused as they were perturbed.

The "tapes" we listened to had some different, presumably still incarnate, narrators—one female, one male—so I was having some separation anxiety from my favorite dead grandpa, Bob Monroe. At least until the end when they gave us a real treat: the final exercise was

147

"classic Bob," culled from the Remote Viewing program. The hemi-sync signals in that one seemed far more potent than all the rest. I experienced a greater opening of my third eye/pineal gland and saw some bright vivid colors, and there were energetic surges so strong I thought I was going to take off! Then I felt my entire energy field flatten like a pancake and spread out to infinity. That was by far the most tripped-out experience I had at Monroe to date.

Leading up to that finale, the exercises were fairly tame—with titles like "Energy Walk," "Body Harmony," "Releasing Fear"—and included forays into chakra clearing, life re-patterning, dolphin healings, and past lives. There were non-CHEC-unit art projects too, like making vision board collages. They had a sea of magazines there for the clipping, spread out over a few big tables. I pored through them seeking magical-mermaid-goddess invoking imagery or really pimpin' home interior shots, and in the process came across a lot of hand sanitizer ads. "Too bad I'm not lookin' to manifest germ-phobia," I joked aloud, but it didn't exactly trigger infectious laughter.

An exercise entitled "Five Questions" was surprisingly fruitful. "*Who Am I?*" was answered for me in a flash with a picture that resembled a multi-faceted amoebic blob, coupled with the instant nonverbal conveyance of "multi-dimensional" and "light." I realize this sounds very generic and cliché. But words cannot do justice, for it truly was a profound moment in which I suddenly and completely understood that there were multiple aspects or personalities or forms to all that is me—a great deal more than this physical body or what the five normal senses are capable of detecting. I was not merely entertaining an intellectual concept. I was provided with a direct feeling of knowing. And it has stayed with me ever since. It's not something I could ever forget or dismiss.

Another question was posed: "*Where and what was I before coming into this body/lifetime?*" This time the response was verbal. I distinctly heard the word "amorous" spoken by a voice I'd never heard before, as if I was suddenly eavesdropping on someone's conversation and that was the particular snippet I'd heard. "We are engaging the dynamism of the inner alchemical process," Karen explained, rather poetically, in one of the debriefing sessions. Hmmm, I liked that. I liked it a lot.

148

Listening to the dolphin healing exercise in my CHEC unit, I started cracking up once the narration began. Maybe the dolphins were tickling me. The exercise wasn't intended as comedy but I found the narrator's voice so outrageous I couldn't stop laughing. He was Rico Suave all the way, over-the-top seductive, slowly and dramatically saying things like "feel the love…," "allow the warmth to penetrate deeply" and "become aware of the rhythm of your body… feel the waves come over you." It was like metaphysical softcore porn.

The next exercise had that same narrator. It was called "Be Earthing/Birthing" and I just did not get it at all. I felt like he was trying to coach me through an OBE or something but I wasn't ready to go there. I fell asleep midway through it, then woke up completely bored by the whole thing and turned it off. When we met in the conference room to debrief, I shared this with the group, because it was very unusual for me to have no interest in an exercise. After a few minutes, a woman named Maria blurted out a confession. She was having difficulty dealing with this "tape" for personal reasons, so she came up with the idea to pretend to be someone else and had selected me because she thought I was happy and impervious to such emotional perturbations. Her crazy scheme had worked: she'd been able to complete the exercise. But now she was stricken with guilt.

I thought it was very funny. I didn't know if her thoughts really influenced me to disconnect like I did, but it was definitely an interesting concept. Her backstory was fascinating but too personal for me to divulge here. The important part is that Maria and I became fast friends and I totally loved her. We felt like long lost sisters, and perhaps we were just that—in another lifetime. They say that it's no coincidence who shows up for these programs together.

The "Past Life Journeys" exercise was another unexpected gift. I'd done past life regressions before, but was always dubious about the results, whether it was me or the practitioner telling the stories. I half-suspected that either I or they were making it all up. But in this hemi-sync session, when I asked a question the answer was delivered to me lightning fast. The most striking one was a scene with an older woman sitting in a dark room alone, sewing. I asked—as prompted by the narrator in my physical ears—when and where she

149

died, and the data was suddenly typewritten before me: 1871 Strasbourg (which I assumed meant France—ironically, the one region I did not visit during last year's trip). I knew that my conscious mind lacked the time and ingenuity to come up with this kind of amazing response, so it felt completely legit. Regardless, the point was clear: I was propagating that same pattern in my current life—living and creating in quiet isolation—and is that what I really wanted? Roger that, higher self.

I think exploring past lives does far more than gratify curiosity. It abets healing and self-growth because these *other* lives (if you care to view them as concurrent) are just different aspects of our total selves. Call me Sybil, but I got some useful insights into my other parts, and therefore my total self, by asking "what's the lesson here?" for each of the characters and life scenes that appeared.

Our group gatherings were low key in contrast to the excited bustle of my former Gateway family. There was a celebrity present (well, at least in certain circles) who sometimes refrained from joining us, making the group even smaller. It was someone I considered very knowledgeable and powerful, and yet in this intimate setting I was peeking into the all-too-human and not necessarily pretty aspects of this person's private life. My lesson was clear: I needed to cease and desist with the black-and-white thinking. Just because people are imperfect and still struggle with personal matters, it need not negate the validity of their teachings or ability to help others. And just in case I didn't grasp the message to let go of the pedestal, it became a theme running through many of my exercises and dreams that week.

There were some other interesting characters present. Like the former Assistant District Attorney who had undergone unsolicited mystical experiences just as she reached the limits of her stress-handling capacity and became a channeler. Another, much older woman had headed up a "dolphin energy healing club," a group of volunteers who send healing thoughts and energies to anyone requesting it, presumably working with and conjuring up dolphins in the process. Oddly, she seemed to be the antithesis of everything I'd ever heard about dolphins, with her stoic and seemingly unplayful demeanor. But I suppose I'd been irrevocably spoiled by those over-the-top Matrix Energetics dolphin frolic-fests.

There was a well-intentioned New Year's Eve party that just sort of fell flat for some of us. The tasty vittles and silly noisemakers were fine, but the last thing I wanted to see was a blaring screen full of Times Square hubbub. It was funny that they did this, considering our first group discussion had revealed that almost everyone was NYE party-averse. Some cultural traditions are inescapable it seems. I ducked out to gaze at the starry skies over Virginia, honoring the new year in my own quiet fashion.

We got to venture into a few focus levels that Gateway hadn't. Level 11, known as "Human Plus" (H-plus) or "the Access Channel," was allegedly Bob Monroe's proudest contribution. It's a level of consciousness that's conducive to profound mind-body healing, where an entrainment of the brain can occur and a mnemonic device can be learned, thereon enabling quick access to the power of altered states from ordinary C1 consciousness.*

By and large, my favorite part of the New Year's Eve program was luxuriating in Focus 18, that pink place of unconditional love. There I found vivid colors and faces, even an angel. Warm fuzzies. I asked, as the guided meditation suggested, "what is my purpose in this lifetime?" That was something I'd been almost dying to know for years. The answer came in the form of a song excerpt. Kurt Elling sang me my answer: "Dedicated to You" and a bright light shone all around. Hey, I'm not making this shit up. I was just observing it, receiving it. It was a great answer, really—simple, yes, but the point is that life is whatever you want it to be. As Neale Donald Walsh says,

---

* H-plus didn't really appeal to me at first, and it seemed way too simplistic to be effective. However, months later I found myself using it with surprising results. I was on a long road trip, getting sleepy with still many miles to go, so I had nothing to lose but my fatigue. I suddenly remembered the tool. I took a deep breath in, held my breath and said to myself "Plus... energy!" then exhaled. Seconds later I was remarkably alert. The proof is in the proverbial pudding. The idea is that the mnemonic can be used with any number of "commands," but "energy" was the one I needed at the time.

there *is* no blackboard in the sky with your preordained purpose scrawled across it.

Right before the exercise wrapped up, I was propelled rapidly backward to my starting point of Focus 18 (where had I been then, if not in 18, I wonder?) The narration culminated with an inspiration to write a personal epitaph. Mine ended up being worded this way:

She learned to truly love herself
and, therefore, everyone else,
and inspired others to do the same.

It doesn't get too much better than that. Thanks Bob.

13

DELUSIONS, PART "DUH"

"Oh love, love, love…
well, that's like hypnotizing chickens."
♫ Iggy Pop

Life in the country was certainly pleasant. Well, aside from discovering that dead mouse upon returning home from the Monroe Institute. The poor thing had been nibbling on a bar of soap in the bathroom sink. I wondered if it was the soap or the lack of food that did him in. Maybe both. It's surprising, the things that inspire you to appreciate your life.

My little nest in Twisp was cozy, but I was becoming restless, socially and intellectually. Oh, I'd made some lovely friends, and there were potlucks and hikes and sometimes plays or live music—it was all quite idyllic on the surface. But I felt disconnected from the community, charming though it was. I suppose part of me always knew that I didn't fit in. The residents with staying power had that deep, fierce connection to Mother Earth, and to physical activity, and I was a mere wannabe, a poser in their midst. In the community center I was both fascinated and petrified to view vintage photos of valley residents ice skating down frozen rivers, as I learned that the mercury sometimes dropped below zero.

Methow Valley life was often vigorous, if not downright toilsome. They wore it like a badge of honor. Many people grew, raised, and preserved their own food, built their own houses, and probably even birthed their own babies too. They wrote the book on DIY (do-it-yourself). I heard exalted tales of people living without electricity or plumbing who would ski in and out of their property to reach the outside world. It was like a new twist on the old Protestant-derived work ethic; whereas the Protestants believed that hard work gets you into heaven when you die, these people were working hard creating their version of heaven on earth. There was a strong reverence for nature, and many people derived great pleasure from what might be viewed as dangerous living—coming into contact with large predator animals, or perhaps narrowly escaping a back-country avalanche while skiing. Playing hard can make you feel that much more alive.

Of course, when I decided to move there, I thought I shared much of these same values with them—well, the locavorism and eco-building at least. I would never be an outdoor jock, try as I may to enlist that fantasy. The local food supply was vastly superior to anywhere else I'd lived, in terms of quality if not variety. I loved walking to the farmers' market and the local butcher shop to procure some bionic veggies or a piece of freshly killed flesh that had been plucked from a nearby pasture. But I was changing... and beginning to see how I was in it for the pure sensory experience of eating fresh food, and less so for the righteousness of local sourcing and a self-sufficient economy. I lacked sufficient motivation to participate actively; I was just lazily enjoying the fruits of other people's labor.

I had moved to Twisp with that old dream still rattling around in my imagination—the one about living on the land—and in savoring the quaint small town life, I saw myself settling down there. Yet in reality, I was leaving the valley nearly every chance I got to attend one woo-woo seminar after the other. For a while I assumed it was just a phase I'd grow out of, and that soon enough I'd simmer down, roll up my sleeves and grab a shovel. I was giving myself a reprieve in order to heal the cyst, with the assumption that my former life of gung-ho material projects would resume once the snow melted.

One problem with that picture was that I wanted a partner to do it all with. God knows, homesteading is difficult enough for a family unit, let alone an individual. There was no way I was going to be okay with becoming a country spinster, especially since I had no matching wacky sister as a cohort (well, that's how it's always done on TV). On the other hand, I wasn't one to wait around for other people to make things happen either.

For a while I considered going in on a piece of land with a new friend in the valley, but she turned out to be emotionally unstable, and our talking never made it to the concrete action stage (whew). Anyway, I wanted a man in my life, but for some reason he just wasn't showing up. It seemed as if all the bachelors in the valley were known... *and* disqualified. But I couldn't readily blame the statistical odds after those magic dates I experienced, post-EFT, in even tinier-town southern Oregon. Nope, the bottleneck had to be *me*.

What to do? I found yet another psychic energy healer and got an appointment, always interested in checking out a new style. This one, Rita, did not employ any brand-name modalities, though she had quite a few tricks in her bag. I called her up with the intention of doing some hypnotherapy, but experienced sticker shock at her price list and opted for a brief intuitive consultation first, in order to get a feel for her personality. Her style was full of tough love, which I normally dig, but it weighed more heavily toward the tough than the love. She called things as she saw them alright, making no attempt to sugar-coat the medicine—or more accurately, the diagnosis, because it didn't feel very solution-oriented. I used to think that the simple act of consciously recognizing my patterns was enough to instigate change. Maybe not, because there she was, reading my energy field and telling me all about my old familiar relationship patterns, as if they were fresh as daisies.

The story went something like this. I had not been treating the men in my life as equals, and I was entering each relationship trying to change them. Basically, I was looking at them as if they were projects. It's not hard to see how this would become problematic. For a little while after the consult, I felt horrible. I beat myself up about it, thinking I must be a real condescending jerk. But then after drifting back to the Mike-story and the game show dream, it dawned on me: hey wait a minute, these guys were NOT my equals! My fundamental error lay in choosing the wrong dudes, in emanating a "come hither, man-project" vibe in the first place, which naturally attracts those who want to be "renovated" (well, at least on some level, whether they know it or not). The ever popular Victim-Savior gag. I knew that I needed to learn greater acceptance in my relationships, but wouldn't it be brilliant to start off with someone who was at least *reasonably* compatible?

Well, okay, now I understood the diagnosis objectively, but that brought me right back to Start: how then could I scour my vibration and break free of the old patterning once and for all? I was not inclined to continue working with Rita. Her hypnotherapy may have done me a lot of good, but I like my healers to feel warm and fuzzy when I'm paying them a nice chunk of change. I didn't linger in the quandary for long though, because a new shiny object caught my eye.

⚡ ⚡ ⚡

Ah, the Interweb, that grand elixir of distraction. I'd dabbled in Internet dating once or twice before, but was never very enthused about it. I had it in my mind that a deep connected relationship could never start that way—for me, that is. Lord knows it's worked magic for all those other people. I knew it was just another tool for the universe to employ, but I just had this stubborn notion about meeting someone organically and having a really good quirky story to tell later on. But maybe those beliefs were self-defeating. Impulsively, I decided to try it again and stay open to possibilities.

At first it was pure entertainment: window shopping at the man-mall and the fun of crafting a profile. But sometimes, on a cold dark winter night, it snuck into the realm of hope, and even flat-out make-believe. Which, come to think of it, is also entertaining. Being as picky as I am, it was rare that I would seriously consider any of the dudes whose profiles I was perusing. And after reading a fair number of them, I couldn't help but notice a trend: most men were deliberately seeking younger women—sometimes up to and including their own age but often dipping way down into the young-enough-to-be-his-daughter range. This started to really piss me off. I don't know why it should, but it did. Maybe because I was still adjusting to the fact that I was over forty and was shocked to realize that I could now be subjected to exclusionary agism. Or perhaps I was peeved because it narrowed the pool even further, as I considered it a red flag and possible indication of character defect.

I decided to conduct a little impromptu survey of the menfolk. I drafted a message in a lighthearted tone, asking for help in solving this little mystery. Out of several dozen surveyed, only four replied. One guy, who I'd already been communicating with, became defensive and insisted that it was completely arbitrary—almost as if the database had filled in the numbers for him. Hmmm.

The second one explained matter-of-factly that he was very youthful. I volleyed, asking "so you don't believe there's an equivalent to you in female form?" His comeback had no game. It seemed like he was suffering from his own version of ye olde inequality relationship pattern, though he wasn't wanting to self-psychoanalyze in the company of a brand new penpal. Can't really fault him for that. The third dude replied briefly in a very positive tone, but said he'd have to get back to me later when he had more time to draft a response. He never did. (I can only assume that everyone gets what they need, and that there was a reason for these interactions, no matter how brief.)

The fourth guy, Mathew, happened to catch me online and started a live chat. He was surprisingly genuine and thoughtful. He explained that he was unsure whether or not he wanted kids, so he figured a younger woman would be the way to go. I asked him why he thought other men did this, even the ones who state they don't want to make any (more) babies. He offered an interesting hypothesis about biological wiring and such, but conceded that some men are simply incorrigible. He didn't even flinch when I pushed things further, asking whether it was fair for men to continue frolicking well into their forties and then decide it's time to procreate, thereby precluding the same freedoms for their female peers. Ultimately we laughed it off and pronounced the issue a supreme joke of nature being played on us all.

The conversation meandered through a variety of topics with such surprising ease and hilarity that I felt pleasantly buzzed when we signed off two hours later and went to sleep a thousand miles apart. It was a surge of energy the likes of which I hadn't felt in years. Who knew such good-natured fun could sprout from an indignant seed?

In the coming days and weeks, more emails were exchanged and he suggested meeting up in person if it were geographically convenient. Since I was already planning to be in San Francisco for some workshops, we arranged a sushi date on his home turf. I didn't put too much weight on it, because I figured the logistics and his propensity for breeding made having a relationship with him strictly impossible. But I was excited at the idea of having an actual proper date. Mainly I was in it for the visceral experience of being in the presence of such a man—a man who seemed markedly different from any I'd ever known. He was simply a prototype in an inconvenient location, and a one-time encounter was all I had in mind. Then I would go back to my cocoon and use that juicy energy to *man*ifest the winning contestant.

I arrived a little early in case I got lost, and found a bench near the restaurant. As I sat there reading, Mathew suddenly appeared before me and I looked up to discover that his photos hardly did him justice. A rapid chemical recomposition of my body was taking place as every cell cried out unanimously, "YES!" Dinner was great and I was more than a little giddy. At some point I realized, as I peripherally scanned the room, that I was laughing too loudly. Oops. But I was having too much fun to reprimand myself for being a dork. Besides, he didn't seem to mind — I was apparently a novelty in his world.

After dinner he drove me to my hotel and came in for a little while, continuing the conversation. It was a swanky place. I'd stayed at a youth hostel the night before, which normally would be fine accommodations, but the one I'd chosen was revolting enough to incite an exodus and a hotel room splurge. My new digs had nice indirect lighting, exposed brick and old-growth wood beams, an iPod player, a couch — a perfectly pimpin' environment for a date.

Not that anything like *that* was about to happen. He was visibly restrained, so I treated the whole thing as if we were just friends hanging out, taking my cue from him in sublimating the strong physical attraction I was feeling. I loved his intelligence and humor. He had a proprietary blend of silly and serious, an ability to talk about deep stuff without becoming emotionally reactive. He seemed to have all the qualities I sought in a man.

Just when things couldn't get any better, Mathew casually mentioned that he used to be a professional swing dance instructor and performer. "WHAT?!?!?" I could not believe my ears. I mean, I really wanted a dancing man, and swing was my favorite style, but I'd figured it was too much to ask of the universe and would've gladly settled for a man with a mere openness to dancing. But here he was essentially telling me that, not only was he *into* it, but he was really f-ing good at it too. It was all over at that point. I asked him to marry me. I thought how fun it would be later on, once the relationship had progressed, to reflect back on the fact that I had proposed on our first date.

It was getting late and it was a school night. Mathew had to work in the morning, and I was leaving town, so we said goodbye with a long sensuous hug. I was effervescing to say the least. But the next day, his words seemed to deflate all the energy that had been built up between us. He was deliberately backing away, choosing logic over emotion. The distance and logistics no longer fazed me—a switch had been thrown. I was infatuated, and when that happens, there can be no insurmountable barriers. I felt like I was in danger of being disqualified from a game I suddenly, intensely wanted to be in and win, even though it was a game unknown to me until a scant twenty hours before. I was scrambling for that opportunity, and I wrote him a long thoughtful letter. He was impressed with my honesty and it served to open up a deeper dialogue and establish a greater level of trust and emotional bonding. I was pleased. I left on a northbound train while exchanging provocative text messages with him.

I wanted to go slow like he did, or at least I thought that's what I should be doing. I knew that my jump-in-with-both-feet method had caused numerous problems in my romantic history, and I was willing to learn a new system. I would let him determine the pace.

We continued the conversation. I looked forward to our phone calls, chats, emails and texts, but did a pretty good job of keeping myself busy otherwise, and keeping my life in balance. Yet I was chomping at the bit to see him again. In most long-distance dating situations, you take turns visiting each other, but I let him off the hook, because I lived in the middle of nowhere and he had just started a new job and had not accrued any vacation time. I knew I was going to have to return to California if I wanted to see him. But I was more than happy to do it, given the gorgeous sunny weather. In fact, I was really starting to warm up to the place in general.

I'd been a Californian once before. Nearly two decades earlier, I drove across country with my minimal possessions in the car, trading one coast for the other in favor of exciting new possibilities and an inexpensive graduate education. There, by the Pacific Ocean, I'd found true love within a week of moving, and in two years we'd gotten hitched. When the two of us left California, I said aloud—to no one in particular, or maybe to anyone who'd listen—that I would *never* live there again. In those days, I was full of piss and vinegar about political outrages, of which the Golden State seemed to have more than its share. (Probably I'd been soaking up too much Jello-Biafra-speak.)

How ironic it was to find myself returning and seeing things through very different eyes—and toying with the idea of moving back.

⚡ ⚡ ⚡

After six weeks of long-distance courtship, I returned to California and cleared my schedule to spend time with Mathew. I imagined long weekends filled with adventures and passionate bliss, hiking, dining, dancing, laughing… and of course, nookie.

Our first date after the hiatus was a little awkward—it felt like we were starting over again. His defenses were back in full force, even more so than before. But we started having fun and laughing, and at the end of the evening I was at his place, sleeping over. It was a somewhat chaste slumber party, filled with warm feelings and laughter, and cast iron restraint on his part. I didn't care; I was just happy to be with him. My openness and bubbly demeanor were visibly wearing him down in a good way, and he became more and more relaxed and responsive.

Then we went swing dancing. I was so excited about the very idea of it that I didn't see the red flag popping up while we got ready to leave: he didn't want to dance with me at home. When we got to the ballroom, it came as a real shock to realize we didn't have dance chemistry. It was awkward. His orientation toward dancing was purely that of a performer, while I was generally entranced by the romance and one-on-one physicality of it all. He was playing to an audience—how strange. Apparently he had been very good at mastering a routine, but less comfortable with spontaneous social dancing.

A few days later, we had another date. This time he had reconstructed his emotional walls so thick, so impenetrable, that there was no chance of retrieving him. I didn't even try. He blurted out the underlying truth: *"I just can't be in a relationship right now."*

I was livid. What the hell was it we'd been doing all this time? Prelude to a lukewarm friendship? This was an outrage! I'd made big plans, and now they were all being flushed down the drain. I left in a huff, and he looked sad and weary. I went back to the hostel where I'd been staying off and on (a nice one this time) and went to bed, feeling rather depressed. The next day my roommate asked me how I was doing. I was in a horrible mood and told her I just had to stew in my own juices for a while, and cautioned her to not take it personally. She was super cool, slightly older than me, and certainly no stranger to the disappointments of life. With a knowing look, she handed me her copy of *The Power of Now* and suggested that I read it.

The book was a welcome distraction from the ugly mechanics of my mind at the moment. I cracked it open and the first line read: "I have little use for the past and rarely think about it." I was intrigued, because at the moment I was strongly disliking my past—especially the very recent past, which looked an awful lot like other scenes from the more distant past.

I read the first chapter straight through. Then the next one, and the next. I couldn't put it down. The more I read, the better I felt. I realized how unnecessary suffering is, and could see very clearly how I'd created it with my own mind. I had obviously been operating in a vacuum—an imaginary version of the future—when I thought about Mathew, and when reality failed to match my bubble, I freaked out. Fortunately, my little temper tantrum only lasted about 24 hours. That had to be an all-time record for me, and I was feeling more than a little self-congratulatory.

I called Mathew and apologized for my childish behavior. He was very understanding. In actuality, he was a mess, just trying to hold himself together and so chock full of fear that it's amazing he was able to let himself be as close to me as he was for the times when he did. I shifted my stance from angry and resentful to compassionate and appreciative, though admittedly I was still pretty sad about the sudden loss of what had seemed like a burgeoning love affair. But there was nothing else I could do but accept the situation; it was out of my hands. And I was kind of okay with it now, thanks to Mr. Tolle.

⚡ ⚡ ⚡

The breakthroughs didn't stop there. Eckhart Tolle's words provoked an internal revolution. The stirrings were already present, but the book's arrival seemed divinely timed to spur the pivotal riot. Well, really that same book had shown up on my doorstep and rang the bell a few times, but *Now* I was ready and willing to let it into the party. My mind was blown wide open, leaving bold new thoughts to breeze through it unhindered.

Mathew had often spoken fondly of his beloved Marin County. It looked and sounded like an ideal place to live and I was quickly becoming enamored of it after spending time there. It had gorgeous undeveloped tracts of land with beaucoup hiking trails, adorable small towns, proximity to the ocean, even a swimmin' hole or two (though none as magnificent as the Methow River could provide) and all this in the backyard of a fabulous, architecturally rich city that seemed to beckon "come dancing!" at every intersection. I'd never thought about living there before. It had never even been on my radar. But now it was looming large, as I revisited my list of priorities. The only caveat was that the place was expensive. There was that money thing.

My relationship with money had been shifting and evolving over the years. I had always been pretty frugal, and in my twenties I considered it a righteous thing to live low on the hog, so to speak. My perspective was tied up in political fervor, striving for some kind of unobtainable absolute equality amongst humans, and I was in the habit of assuming that wealthy people were unscrupulous. Throughout my thirties, I slowly released that garbage, through a series of personal experiences custom designed for learning just that. By the time I met Mathew, I was feeling pretty neutral about other people having money, so I had no particular allergic reaction to the overt wealth of Marin, but I was still wrestling with the tricky task of giving myself permission to be wealthier. Living there would be a big leap into a higher-end lifestyle. My nest egg wasn't what it used to be, and I still dreamed of owning another house someday.

But that was fear talking. I thought back to my early twenties —how little money I'd had and how little I worried about it. It seems that the older we get, the more we have and the more scared we are of losing it. Fear was largely what inspired me to move to the country in the first place: fear that society was going to hell in a handbasket, fear that the economy was about to implode. Fear of survival, really. Fear of not having enough; fear of something horrible happening; fear of being surrounded by too many people who would not adapt well to the coming changes; fear of negative energy infiltrating me. Fear of the government taking away civil liberties; fear of an anarchistic state; fear of fascism. Blah, blah, blah... *fear!* Fuck fear.

For all I know, the world *is* going down the tubes and the economy *is* going to implode, and we all *are* going to be clubbing each other over the head to get at the subsistence grubs, but it's just plain irrelevant to my current reality. Que sera, sera. I will deal with whatever happens when it happens. So what if the voyeuristic paranoid government or opportunistic marketeers are scanning my every conversation and email? I've got nothing to hide or fear. I just want to be happy, dammit. I recalled Joseph Campbell's profound advice and decided it was high time I started following my true unobstructed bliss, now that I'd cleaned the mud off of it.

I really missed partner dancing since I'd left Portland, but I'd told myself the lie that it didn't matter. Growing food and becoming self-reliant seemed far more important—survival was serious business, and frivolity was a low priority. (Sheesh, I sounded like my uptight ancestors.) I'd been living for the Future. Worse yet, I'd been living in fear of a Future I didn't even like. How liberating it was to come to terms with all of this! I was finally able to admit to myself that I really did not want to bust my hump building an eco-house and toiling on the land. Doing everything the hard way was a big part of my Past, but now I could drop that torch. I was genuinely ready to live in the Now. Tingly sensations flowed through me as I silently repeated my new mantra: "Yes, I *can* have it all!" (Well, nearly all. I would miss that Methow Valley goat cheese... sigh.)

It was time for me to re-emerge into a more populated area. I was past the point of worrying about how other people's energy might affect me. I'd gotten to where I could maintain my own energy fairly consistently, regardless of who or what was around me. I still wasn't wanting to live in a dense urban setting, but Marin provided the perfect happy medium to satisfy both the country mouse and the city mouse in me. All I had to do was pony up some extra cash for rent, and slay one last dragon in the process: that fearful voice who worries aloud in my head about running out of money. That tired old scarcity show that keeps finding its way in the back door, even after being kicked off the stage countless times. But I could beef up security. I was determined to remain conscious of my own mind—and wise to the tricks it plays—once and for all. Eckhart, I think I got it!

⚡ ⚡ ⚡

Mathew and I stayed in touch for a short while, attempting to maintain some semblance of a friendship, but it seemed forced and unnecessary so I let it fade away. I was grateful for the huge service he'd provided in inadvertently helping me identify and release a boatload of fear. Which was highly ironic because he seemed so overrun with it himself. Likely the power lay in the mirror he held up before me; I gasped at my reflection and immediately went to work.

The relationship derailment was a proverbial blessing in disguise (and I suppose anything can be, if you gaze at it through the proper spectacles). It's wild to look back on the master plan, post-execution—that plot twist I never saw coming. This cute guy waltzed into my life straight out of the cyber-ethers, swept me off my feet, and showed me around my soon-to-be new homeland, graciously opening the door and then promptly slamming it, thereby shattering my remaining major life-illusions. I suppose they'd already been reduced to a fragile thin pane, since I'd slogged through the lion's share of auto-chicanery after the last romantic debacle. Still, this was quite a novel sensation to be in a state of honest awe and appreciation—rather than disdain—for my own crafty delusions. I marveled at the crucial role misplaced passion had played in precipitating my next big step, while vowing to not require such extreme prodding from the puppet masters in the future.

A few weeks later I happened upon the hilarious book *He's Just Not That Into You*. Ah, yes, it was all making sense now. My powers of romantic self-deceit were quite impressive and I'd been completely immersed in my character role, but now I had the writer-director's vantage point.

Soon I was back in Twisp, getting ready for yet another epic adventure involving a moving truck. It was time to let go of all my tools and tiles and implements of construction. I knew it was the right thing to do, but it amounted to a mini emotional ordeal nevertheless. Not so much because of the money I'd spent acquiring those things— after all, it was just stuff and replacements could be found, should a need arise—but because I was molting again. A huge part of my former identity was falling away and I wasn't sure what might take its place. I was no longer a Sawz-all owning, pipe wrench slinging bad-ass chick; I had grown soft. And yet, I was happy about it, excited to be cracking open a brand new chapter. Transitions are always a mixed bag, but liberating some material behemoths helped propel me onward and upward.

As I packed up my things in my cute apartment, I came across an old notebook in which I'd written a list of ideal man-qualities. I was amazed at just how precisely Mathew measured up. But I'd omitted a few petty little demands to the universe—like emotional availability, for instance. It pays to be specific and thorough in doing the visioning... and then flexible and open, but also very *discerning*, in doing the receiving. At any rate, I was thrilled because I remembered just how true and potent all that Law of Attraction stuff really is. I had deliberately manifested things before—stuff, people, situations—with great success, but in this dense and challenging world, a gal can stand a lot of reminding and reinforcing.

14

SPOON BENDING
AND
HORMONAL CONTENTION

"Things I once thought unbelievable
in my life have all taken place."
♫ P. J. Harvey

At last! I was back in Virginia at the Monroe Institute and spoon bending was imminent. I could not *wait* to get my hot little hands on some silverware and hopefully, under the proper tutelage, I'd be bending that sucker six ways from Sunday with just sheer Vulcan mindpower. Then I'd have the ultimate souvenir to bring home. Some people yearn to conquer mountains or bungee jump into deep canyons, but to me, mangling flatware was somehow the pinnacle of human accomplishment. The promotional literature baited: "an adventure in consciousness that helps make your dreams come true." It also touted acts of growing seeds faster, influencing computers and dice, illuminating light bulbs, and other superhuman feats.

Over the years I'd met a few people who told me they had bent spoons, usually in some hippie circle back in the '60s or '70s. I was simultaneously exhilarated and incredulous as I listened intently to their stories. It's not that I didn't believe them (they seemed like perfectly sane human beings) but telekinesis just teetered on the magical and near-impossible end of things, even though I wanted so badly to experience it myself. It seemed like spoon-bending had been a fad that all but faded—like so many rollerskating rinks in the '80s— but perhaps it was time for a revival now that we humans appeared to be emerging from our collective-limitation stupor. Fast forward to 2011: fashion has called for the replacement of the term "telekinesis" with the newer hipper "psychokinesis" or PK.

I know it's popular to believe that Uri Geller (the well known spoon bender of yore) was a phony, but that's not unlike those small but vehement groups of revisionists who claim certain historical events never happened. Ask someone who was *there* what happened. Personally, I choose to respect the people who say "yup, it did happen, and I saw it myself" so it makes sense to me that Geller either deliberately faked his famous failure in order to take the heat off himself and disappear into a more private life, or that he simply couldn't replicate the act on demand every time. And if reality is subjective as the physicists say it is, it's possible for several people to be in the same place at the same time and observe different things.

Anyway, I think when people have a strong negative reaction to something like this it's because they're experiencing fear. That is, their intellectual prowess is being challenged, so a typical line of defense is to ridicule the uncomfortable subject. It's a very human thing to do, but you can miss out on a lot that way. I suppose some just prefer their realities on the predictable side while others, such as myself, crave heterodoxy. Either way, it all boils down to "seeing is believing" and I was about to see for myself what was possible.

⚡ ⚡ ⚡

A slight hassle had ensued while checking in at the airport. The ticket-bot machine was pretending that I never even booked a flight, and the agent seemed surly at first—more interested in chatting with his co-workers than addressing my pesky little customer service issue. "We don't *have* a 6:40 flight," he told me flatly. What? Did I have the wrong day or something? Ah, so maybe that's why my friend who dropped me off said she'd wait to make sure everything was okay —perhaps she was psychically tuning in to some SNAFU that was about to happen. My natural response to her was "of course everything's fine, why wouldn't it be?" I don't relate to worry. My mother is probably to thank for this, because unlike other moms who insist that you call when you arrive, she would leave me with this sentiment: "well, if something happens, I'm sure I'll hear about it on the news."

I remained patient and calm; it was too early to be anything but docile anyway. The agent started to soften. I've seen this sort of thing happen before and it's a fun little game I like to play with disgruntled service workers. I just remember that they're beautiful people who've been beaten down by the onslaught of ornery demanding customers and probably obnoxious management as well, getting squeezed on both sides. One time I had a woman thank me profusely—apparently an amicable customer was rare in her world.

The agent rolled up his sleeves and solved the problem. Walking away, feeling happy and light after relinquishing my big ol' suitcase, I silently and deliberately vowed that for the rest of my trip, I would have only positive experiences and come upon as many "lightworkers" as possible. That's what I call the people who stand out

169

with their sunny demeanors, serving and relating to the larger world with love. They may be holding any kind of job, but there is a certain unmistakable light in their eyes. They're always out there, of course, but I have to be in the right frame of mind to be able to rendezvous with them.

My plan took effect immediately. While I waited for my carry-on bag and shoes to emerge on the conveyer, the federal security guy asked me if I needed a shoehorn. For a moment I was sleepily thinking "wow, now *that's* service" until I realized he was joking. "I'm a Shoehorn," his stand-up routine continued, "I'm Native American." (He actually did look like he had Native blood in him.) He grabbed a Ziploc bag full of liquids and gels and held it up while loudly faux-scolding us. "Look, this guy knows the TSA rules! Everybody, take notes from him!" The baggie's owner, a conservative-looking business traveler, looked slightly mortified. Ever since 911, we've been well-trained to not only remove humor from the airport entirely, but to become flinchy and nervous at the mere thought of it.

En route to the gate, I strolled alongside the businessman. "You don't *ever* see a TSA guy having fun like that!" I reveled. "Never!!" he agreed in total amazement. Did that really just happen, or had the whole scene been conjured up by the universe for our amusement? All I knew was that it was only 6:00 am and there would be many more humorous and heart-warming incidents before I made my way to Bob Monroe's place in the Blue Ridge Mountains.

⚡ ⚡ ⚡

The MC² (Manifestation and Creation Squared) program had been on my calendar for quite some time, and I would have jumped right in if it weren't for the fact that I had to take the introductory Gateway Voyage first*. Having been at the Institute months earlier only served to increase my giddy anticipation because they had these

---

* For your information, the prerequisite has since been eliminated. However, for me, Gateway turned out to be the best thing since sliced bread.

display cases of bent spoons and forks in the common areas, ripe for the ogling.

When people start filtering in on the first day of a residential program, they tend to congregate and mingle where the snacks and drinks are, so I went down there to meet and greet my new classmates. Continuing the steady social decline from my ecstatic Gateway brat pack to the lukewarm New Year's Eve group, the MC^2 attendees seemed like the most socially awkward subset of humanity I'd ever encountered. They were mostly not speaking to one another, while sitting around the table in close proximity, like a dysfunctional family (unlike my own which was never the silent type unfortunately). The ones who did speak kinda made me wish they hadn't. There was a guy who hated his corporate life and acted like a victim with a pension-package-gun held to his head. And a woman rattling off a list of meds she was currently taking or was being persuaded by her doctor to start taking. Another one would blurt out non-sequiturs of "have you read ____?" and when no one responded with any indication of interest, she took this as her cue to launch into greater detail.

I was shocked. This motley crew had come to perform magic and miracles? How in tarnation could they influence the molecules of a metal object when they seemed to lack any sizable semblance of control over their own personal lives? I know that sounds very judgmental, but I was honestly floored and puzzled as to how this PK stuff was going to work. I guess I'd taken on an erroneous belief that the really powerful people were like ascended masters who had long surpassed the limits of mundane struggle. Which is not to say that I myself fit that bill. I wasn't really sure how I was going to pull off the spoon-bending either. I was relying on blind faith in the program, because I thought so highly of the Monroe Institute.

More characters. There was an older gentleman from South Carolina, a physician, who I later took to avoiding because his narcissism was such a drag, and his spoutings revealed a not-so-thinly-veiled racist outlook on life that I found distasteful. I'm hardly a proponent of political correctness, but it was embarrassing to be within earshot of this guy. At first, I was curious to hear how he reconciled his obvious interest in The Weird with his mainstream vocational activity as an M.D.—curious enough to suffer the indignity of his company and interview him straightaway. Unfortunately, he just skirted the question and headed off on an uninteresting tangent.

There was a fifty-something woman named Wendy who reminded me of the Muppets, as she was animated and bouncy with a mop-like head of hair. Actually, she looked like a carbon copy of Karla, the woman who had once given me that *I Am Worthy!* CD. But Wendy was much perkier. She had none of the tortured-childhood canvas that Karla was painting on. They could have been twins separated at birth, one adopting the belief that it was perfectly okay to be dorky, while the other got the idea that it was somehow problematic. Word got out that Wendy was a singer, and she was heartily encouraged to sing out, loud-n-proud at will, as part of the raise-your-energy aspect of the program. The only problem with that plan was that Wendy's bliss was somehow inversely proportional to mine. She literally was belting out "Hallelujah!" at regular cringe-tastic intervals, sounding just like that Church Lady character from Saturday Night Live.

So much for positivity. My Pollyanna momentum had been derailed. It was an inauspicious start for sure, but I figured I would just go about my business and delve into the exercises. What I didn't know was that the program was heavily dependent upon *group bonding*.

One night at dinner, I was trying to make lemonade, so to speak, because the group was so small that there weren't a lot of options as far as tables to sit at or people to talk with. It was clearly going to be an all-or-nothing social situation. While we ate, I brought up the topic of energy healing, since it was going to be part of the program. At some point I explained that I'd been learning some different healing modalities and would be happy to use them on any willing guinea pigs. Martha, a woman in her fifties with the emotional maturity of a damaged-goods teenager, replied with a scoff that she herself was, in fact, an energy healer and that she would definitely *not* be needing my services. "Oh-kaay…," I thought. She was precisely the sort of character Eric Pearl has a field day with. There was something about the tone of her voice that always sounded sarcastic and disdainful, regardless of what she was saying.

Also in attendance was a gay couple, Allan and Rolland, whom I genuinely liked. They were my saving grace. Allan was extremely introverted and shy, while Rolland was his polar opposite—gregarious and outgoing as can be. I probably exchanged a total of ten words with Allan, but learned much about him through his chatty adoring partner. Then, rounding out the strange mix was an actual honest-to-goodness awkward acne-faced teenager. He said virtually nothing all week, speaking only when it was absolutely necessary. He was so skilled at fading into the background that I almost forgot he was there most of the time. Hmmm, I could learn a lot from that kid.

After the meal, Bob, a heavy-set sixty-year-old man with shifty eyes and a perma-frown, approached me and gave me a little sob story about the terrible headache he was suffering, asking if I would be willing to do some energy work on him. Even as he spoke I detected insincerity, but in a knee-jerk reaction I agreed, because I'd just publicly made the offer to the entire group. Besides, what's the harm in it? I usually learned something interesting by practicing this stuff on someone new. Having someone feign illness was, in fact, a new experience for me as a pseudo-practitioner.

We agreed to meet in the den where Bob could lie down on the couch. I did my energy healing thing, which is less of a routine and more of an amalgamation of various techniques intuitively woven together on the spot. Sometimes I "invent" new ones as I go. When the session felt complete, I let him know, and asked him what he experienced—the standard debriefing. Usually my "clients" remain still for a few minutes as they come back into full consciousness, then recount some interesting sensations, feelings, or visions that occurred. Not Bob. He sprang up immediately, announced that his headache had completely vanished, and before I could even respond, he was giving me a hug. A creepy, too-long and too-close-for-comfort hug. Ew. Although I wasn't physically harmed in any way, I felt energetically violated. It was obvious to me in that moment that he had for sure lied, and that I'd just been psychically sucker-punched for a cheap thrill.

I was feeling angry because I'd paid a lot of money to attend the program, and playing with subtle energies required the letting down of my energetic guard (or so I thought). It was the same sort of predicament as that Theta Healing class when the instructor violated personal boundaries, although in this case, it wasn't clear that I needed to let my guard down in order to achieve the desired results of the program. But it had happened nonetheless, and I was feeling very weirded out and unable to snap out of it.

I spoke to the trainers. Not that there was anything to be done, really. I'm not a fan of litigiousness or patriarchal (or matriarchal) rule. I guess I just wanted them to understand my conundrum so they would know why I was feeling so disconnected. Really, I was starting to get damn cranky in general, and things just seemed to be getting worse by the minute. My hormones were in the driver's seat, and they were swerving all over the road.

As co-creator of my life, I naturally had to question myself. Why this, why now, when I'd been so looking forward to this week? Was I getting an education in creative negligence? I'd been pretty laissez-faire about my impending experience, not having spent much time envisioning it (or "segment intending" as the Abraham-Hicks jargon goes—more on that soon). I had simply slapped down the tuition and sauntered in there, presuming that everything would magically work out, as it often does. But why had it gone so horribly awry this time? And why couldn't I just right my course, midstream? The negative funk I was in was so extreme, it was absurd. Surely there must have been a mix-up on the part of my cosmic waitress. I ordered a lesson in spoon-bending, not button-pushing, dammit.

Puzzled and crabby, all I could do was go back to placing blame with the hormones. At times I've felt like there was a very real but invisible army invading my bloodstream, and that I was under siege, completely floundering until they chose to split town a few days later (presumably via my uterus, using gravity—those brilliant little escape artists). It amounted to a Jekyll and Hyde production I was starring in, usually about once a month. But the current showing was an unexpected encore performance, with more vim and vigor than ever before. I was hemorrhaging like crazy after a mere two-week hiatus from the last bloodletting. Maybe all the travel I'd been doing was placing extra stress on my body? Or maybe it was a symbolic form of grieving over my recent relationship-that-wasn't with Mathew?

Even under somewhat normal conditions, my female ritual could be a scary-clown carnival with all-you-can-eat junk food and unlimited rides on the rickety emotional roller-coaster. But usually I had the luxury of retreating into my own self-amusement park and locking the gates—so no one gets hurt. Now, at TMI, without the option of crawling into a cave, the timing was terribly inconvenient. It was tempting to literally stay cozied up in my CHEC unit all week and avoid the button-pushers altogether, but after all the self-imposed hype, I wasn't willing to forfeit the psychokinetics in favor of what would amount to an overpriced country respite. No, the show must go on, I decided.

⚡ ⚡ ⚡

Like most Monroe programs, MC² made use of hemi-sync technology, and we visited Focus Levels 11, 12, 15, and 21. Some exercises were just "metamusic" tracks (music plus hemi-sync signals) that we'd listen to with a specific intention. In between CHEC unit exercises was a great deal of group activity—far more than my other TMI experiences. It seemed that synergistic energy is the key to psychokinesis, at least initially for the beginners.

We did some generic manifesting work via writing, meditation, affirmations and the like, culled from various sources including Abraham-Hicks material. There were "healing circles" where we'd take turns laying in the center. When it was my turn to have the others hurl their good intentions at me, I found it a bit unnerving; it didn't feel soothing or healing at all. My thoughts went back to Eric Pearl's objection that too many cooks spoil the energetic broth. I think he's got a point there.

The first of the psychokinetic experiments was dice-rolling. Before rolling, it was crucial to raise your vibrational level in order to achieve above-average results. The trainers suggested a few methods: some more meditative and subtle; some entailed creating a ruckus in the room, playing music, dancing, whooping it up, hugging each other.

One by one, each person announced an intention to throw a particular roll—say, six, in any combination of the two dice. After ten rolls, the results were tallied and compared to statistical probabilities. There was no doubt about it—people were beating the odds. The trainer's results were most impressive of all—a good sign of competence. Obviously, this held exciting implications for winning money, and they actually have conducted a similar program in Las Vegas with great success. Yes, PK was clearly working.

Except... not for me. I grew more prickly with each roll of the dice. The happier and goofier everyone else became, the more I felt like running far, far away. The blaring lame classic rock tunes and Wendy's exuberant singing were not helping. When it was my turn to roll the dice, some of them hugged me, which was awkward—it felt like another violation of my personal space. I made a feeble attempt to raise my own vibration by putting on headphones with music that I like, but there was no use. It was like trying to lift a bulldozer with a feather. My results stank; they were worse than the statistical average. I was temporarily back in fourth grade on a school bowling trip, throwing gutter ball after gutter ball. Only the spotlight was wider this time, and they all cheered me on, Special Olympics style, as they'd done for everyone else. This flock of oddballs was genuinely trying to love me up, but I just wasn't having any of it.

There was an experiment with seed-growing, following some discussion and a short film about Dr. Emoto's famous work with thought-forms and water crystals. Interesting stuff.*

The days went on and I felt pretty much the same. I made more half-hearted but ultimately futile attempts to raise my vibrational state by skipping out on some of the group sessions, taking walks in the woods, staying in my room dancing to music. When I was doing these things I was happy, but when I reconvened with the group, it was right back to annoyance central. I kept stepping on to Planet

---

* Later, at the end of the program, the little bowls of sprouted seeds were paraded around and, indeed, some were noticeably larger than others, due to the pure love energy that had been projected into them. Anyone who works with plants understands that we humans affect them with our intentions and energy. It will come as no surprise to hear that my seedlings looked pathetic.

Dork and wondering why it stubbornly refused to transform itself into Planet Bliss.

Another day's PK trick involved lighting up round fluorescent tubes with our hands, rather than the usual electricity and light fixtures. We engaged in some preparation to build up energy once again, then they handed out the light bulbs and darkened the room. As we each held onto our glass tubes with both hands, it only took a minute for some of them to light up. The trainer had his going faster and brighter than most. It was impressive, if not long-lasting. Some of them seemed to pulse on and off a bit, the way fluorescent bulbs look when they reach the end of their life cycles. Mine remained darkened. Perhaps I'd been issued a dud? Maybe. But highly unlikely. I knew of course that the real dud was my attitude. I remained like a caged animal lashing out, incapable of grabbing the keys to the cage... but periodically relinquishing the fight in favor of a good nap.

⚡ ⚡ ⚡

Eventually, the big day arrived. Silverware contortion! Our chairs were arranged in a circle, and in the center was a big pile of spoons and forks on the floor. We dove in excitedly and returned to our seats with some choice specimens. I selected some fancy old ones made of real silver, but then I wondered if I should have picked something more flimsy and pliable like cheap cafeteria-style flatware. But then, it shouldn't matter, since it wasn't about brute force. I deemed the little deco rosettes my good-luck charms, as I was still—or again—hopeful with possibilities at this point.

Our trainer described two different approaches. First, the "yin" method. This involved sitting quietly, gathering energy within oneself, holding the spoon or fork lovingly, stroking it, perhaps talking to it, asking it to conform to our wishes, quietly projecting energy into it. A few people were able to create a slight bend in the metal using this method.

Next was the "yang" method, and Planet Dork swung into high gear. Here's how it was done: overt energy-raising via all means necessary, then, while holding the spoon or fork, projecting all that

177

focused energy into it in a split-second while yelling "BEND!!" at the thing. This truculent command was accompanied by violent jumping and gesturing. It wasn't really my style. I suppose the "yin" method could have been fruitful, had I been in the proper vibrational state. But for nearly everyone else, the "yang" method was an unqualified success.

I literally saw spoons and forks bending, warping, tangling all around me! Some people were on a roll and bent several in a row. Some of the bends were simple, looking like the spoon had just slumped over, while others were elaborate masterpieces with fork tines curled in multiple directions. Several people started spontaneously parading around the circle, showing off their work by literally putting it in everyone else's face. To them, I'm sure it felt triumphant, but to me and probably to the only other person who was getting bupkis for results (the teenager), it came across as irritating at best, and competitive at worst.

Time seemed to stand still while I watched Rolland contorting his fork. And yet, it was all over so quickly, just like the lightbulb exercise. I was thinking that if I could have had just a little more time, maybe, just maybe... eh, who was I kidding? I saw what it took and I was nowhere near the required state of mind.

Before attempting the spoon-bending ourselves, we had watched a video of prior program participants. Some of them said they couldn't do it during the group exercise but it happened later on, sometimes unexpectedly—somehow the energy was delivered to the spoon after a lag time, like a piece of mail that emerges from a dead letter office. So I took my unmolested flatware back to my CHEC unit, just in case. It was more likely to happen when I was happier and high-vibrating, and that meant being away from this group. But I was also concerned that the collective resonance was a necessary ingredient.

The irony of the whole situation was incredibly thick. Feeling happy and upbeat is my default modus operandi, but this week had been a major falling-off-the-wagon anomaly. I hit an all-time vibrational low, just when it mattered most. Meanwhile, other people who seemed relatively miserable in their everyday lives took a vacation, let loose, and performed magic. Was it because they were able to summon all that pent-up "hate my boss" energy and pitch it at the spoons? If only I could have garnered a critical mass of "leave me the fuck alone" energy and focused it on a fork...

Seriously, though, getting happy and being immersed in the moment is the twofold key, I think, when it comes to psychokinetic endeavors. The less thinking and analyzing (and doubting) that goes on, the better and quicker the results.

Well, it was an impressive show, and I learned a thing or two, even if my own participation was a wash. I was still hung up on finding a reason why things went the way they did. I asked myself if there was some hidden fear undermining my conscious intentions. Perhaps a fear of being in the limelight, like Uri Geller, and feeling the pressure to perform? That thought definitely made me uncomfortable, but was it a realistic scenario? If I was harboring fear along those lines, it had to be coming from someplace much deeper, far older. You know, like from some former life as a witch getting burned at the stake. Perhaps my button-pushing companions were newer kids on the earth-block, so they didn't have any ancient fear-baggage like that to interfere with their whooping-it-up. Well, it was a theory anyway.

At least I wasn't feeling inferior. I figured we all have the same "equipment" as humans, so if others could enact such feats, certainly I could too under the right conditions. I left the program thinking that someday, when I'm in the company of people I love and we're splitting our sides laughing like we often do and vibrating off the chart, that's when I'll pull out some silverware and get busy.

Aside from the unsolicited lessons in acceptance, I received an unexpected gift during the program week. It seemed like a minor thing at the time, but later proved to be momentous. Rolland and I took a walk to Lake Miranon one day during an afternoon break. It was a crisp sunny day and we entertained ourselves and each other chatting about all sorts of esoteric and funny stuff. I learned Rolland's charmingly obtuse method of answering that old pesky question "what do you *do*?" He would say "Nothing. Well... except breathing. I know I shouldn't *really* need to, but I haven't figured out yet how to do that." I loved his outlandish sense of humor and admired his ability to remain impervious to his surroundings. He was no more fond of the dorklings than I was, but it just didn't bother him at all, and his results spoke volumes. But then, he didn't have a contentious uterus.

Out of the blue, while we sat lazily in the sun gazing at the lake, Rolland asked me if I'd ever considered writing a book. I was surprised because I hadn't revealed much that would have led to this conclusion. I suppose he used his spidey sense. I had been churning out a good deal of writing, but couldn't see a way of assembling it cohesively enough to give it widespread appeal or usefulness until then. When we returned to the Institute, I stopped in the little library and certain books started popping out. Ideas starting coming. The inspiration continued into my dreams and meditations until I finally knew I was going to write this book and could conceive of how to structure it. So, ultimately my MC^2 program was a fruitful one, even if the fruit tasted sour and unripe at the time. I thought I was going there for some mango sorbet but it turned out to be a blueberry cobbler. (Or something like that.)

⚡ ⚡ ⚡

On my way out of town, I stopped in the metaphysical bookshop in Charlottesville. It was a sweet little mother-and-daughter operation (though the two looked more like sisters). Somewhere between Barbara Hand Clow and Byron Katie, I struck up a conversation with a guy named Alexander Duncan Cameron. He was there to give a talk about his experiences with time travel, having been part of the famous but mysterious and controversial "Philadelphia Experiment" (not the movie, but the actual project). I recalled Richard Bartlett talking about it—allegedly the government had successfully de-materialized a giant ship then re-materialized it many miles away. Well, apparently, there were people on board, and this fellow was one of them.

To be honest, I know almost nothing about that Experiment, but I've got to say that when I looked into the man's light blue eyes, there was something about him that was very very *different*, as if he was more porous, more like a light-body than the rest of us. He looked to

180

be about sixty years old, but the math simply didn't add up—he ought to be much, much older. In other words, the implication is that the man had spent some significant time (from our perspective) where there *is* no time. Freaky.

While perusing the books I discovered a fantastic little paperback called *The Handbook for Perfect Beings*. I first opened it to a random page and read the following passage: "be aware of what you ask for. If you've asked for more patience, you're going to have more people around that irritate you." Hmmph. I couldn't recall putting patience near the top of my wishlist. Maybe some mischievous spirit guides had played a practical joke and rearranged the list while I was sleeping. I'd much rather have them rearrange my hormones.

A few weeks later, I had the most remarkable experience. I'm not sure what prompted it, but I had this sudden understanding—as if by cosmic download—that, while I had been acting like a hapless victim bobbing in a sea of raging hormones, *I* was the one who was truly in charge. It wasn't a conscious thought or decision; it just came to me loud and clear, unrelated to my preceding thoughts. I suddenly understood that I could call the shots. A simple concept, but one I hadn't actually fully engaged in before.

I'd always been looking for outside assistance. But it seemed that every "alternative" healer I asked would say the same thing: there's not much to be done. Worse yet, they would start talking about conventional medical procedures and artificial hormonal solutions, which is about the last thing I wanted to hear. It seemed to me that if we could assert our influence over the molecular structure of an "external" object such as a metal spoon, surely we could master the inner organic workings of our own bodies. Yet I was being told repeatedly that it wasn't possible or feasible, by people whose healing abilities and wisdom I had previously held in high regard. It just didn't make a whole lot of sense.*

But now... *now* my mind had just been infused with this stalwart knowing. I got quiet and meditated, then had a little chat with the members of Team Babymaking Machine. I said "hey, I know you've been working hard for a long time and I really appreciate that, but guess what? The project's been cancelled! Woohoo! That means early retirement, so take a rest, go to Tahiti and have lots of fun, why don't you? Thanks a lot." After that, I did not see hide nor hair of ye olde bleeding ritual for a record six months (I guess they got bored with Tahiti after a while).   Wow, maybe that spoon-bending extravaganza did inspire me to wield more personal power, but in a more practical application? Well, in case I ever qualify for flashier work, I'm keeping some silverware handy.

---

* Months later, I met a woman who had taken the MC^2 course at Monroe. She had successfully bent spoons, both during the program and afterward, alone and with non-spoon-bending friends present in the comfort of her own home, which was great to hear because it dispelled my concern that group energy was required. She told me about a chronic health problem she was suffering from and I asked whether she could use her superpowers to change it. She replied, "oh... I never thought about it."

15

VORTEX OF ATTRACTION

"Your words run through me
like the blood in my veins."
♫ Lucinda Williams

Vortex of Attraction. Sounds like a dating game, eh? Actually it was the latest term for the Esther Hicks, Jerry Hicks and Abraham traveling show, variously known in the past as the "science of deliberate creation" or the "art of allowing" and probably a few other catch phrases as well.

I'd seen *The Secret* when it first came out and remembered especially liking Esther Hicks and what she had to say, though admittedly I was confused about the different names, thinking that Abraham Hicks was her dead dad or former husband or something. I hadn't paid particular attention to the small but telling hyphen in "Abraham-Hicks" and the film didn't do much to explain it either. After giving them no further thought in the intervening years, one of those seemingly random inspirational flashes had me looking at their website and registering for a workshop in San Francisco.

The seminar was another one of those five hundred people in the packed hotel ballroom kinda things, but much more normal than a Matrix Energetics seminar. That is, if you consider a sixty-year-old woman channeling a group of spirit entities named Abraham *normal*. Esther herself does not use the term "channeling" to describe the phenomenon she participates in, but it's probably just a matter of semantics.*

I'd witnessed live channeling before, so it didn't strike me as particularly strange. I had recently dragged a friend along to see Barbara Marciniak, having found parts of her book *Earth* to be compelling. Before the talk officially began, Marciniak and her fans chatted excitedly about chemtrails and alien power conspiracies. I was mildly bored by what seemed like fear-based fervor in the room, but my friend was becoming visibly uncomfortable. She was a good sport though, and agreed to stay. It was an opportunity to practice the art of parsing out message and messenger—because there are pearls to be gleaned if you allow the emotional reactions to subside. Even if you

---

* After watching her many times, I could easily see the transformation that comes over her when she "merges," if you will, with Abraham. It's not a phony act, though I can understand why other people might think so— probably for fear of being taken for a ride or of being perceived as someone who gets taken for a ride.

don't believe in channeling per se, you can still listen to the content and decide whether or not it's useful. It's like agreeing to disagree with someone — only, that someone is you. Or maybe it's like using the Dr. Bronner's soap despite the weirdo rap on the label. Adventures in baby bathwater.

Despite the fear-mongering, I was able to extract one enormous gift from that book and those Pleiadians (the ones Marciniak channels, known colloquially as "the Ps"). It was about the nature of Gaia, the powerful feminine energy surrounding or governing our Earthly existence. I'd been thinking about that sort of "lost feminine" notion because of my fascination with energy healing, and had gotten this bee in my bonnet that there was an epoch in human history when hands-on healing was everyday household stuff, widely accepted as real and effective, but that over the millennia we shifted to a masculine-based culture and eradicated nearly every trace of our old fabulous witchy ways. Whether I was tapping into some long-forgotten knowledge or romanticizing the past, I don't really know. It was just a kick I was on. Either way, when I read Marciniak's words about *allowing* as the very mother-like energy, the *yin* principle, something clicked in a big way.

I felt relieved. And full of acceptance. Not just of the things happening in my personal life, but of the big picture. For once, I could sense a master plan of some sort. I mean, I'd always hoped and believed there must be one, but I hadn't been clear on what it might be. It dawned on me that what seems like utter chaos in the world is absolutely, unequivocally OKAY because all things are *allowed* in this giant elaborate petri dish. Things are always changing and evolving, and the mess we're in will work itself out. Or maybe it isn't even a mess at all. It's a matter of perspective. Just as a mother loves her children no matter how wretched they may become, a goddess would love everything that happens here. I realized I could borrow that point of view, and I rather liked the idea of thinking like a goddess. Life is literally "all good" — perfect in its imperfection. It wasn't so much that Marciniak's book convinced me of anything; it was more like a pipe wrench on a stuck-shut valve. There was already a reservoir of well-being within me but it hadn't been as free-flowing as it could be.

No longer did I need to schlep around that big iron chain of disbelief and suspicion about goodness in the world—the gigantic question mark about why we're here. (I was still a little shaky on why I in particular was here, but that too would soon be revealed.) Exposure to Theosophy had helped to prime me for this insightful turning point, which in turn set the stage for my next big revelation.

⚡ ⚡ ⚡

Like many savvy New Age dabblers, I thought I already understood the Law of Attraction (LOA) and wondered how it was possible that so many thousands of hours of Abraham-Hicks workshops had been logged covering this one simple topic. I got that thoughts are powerful, and that I am essentially a living breathing transmitter and receiver of vibrations. The manifesting process seemed ridiculously simple: focus on what you want and believe it, then it's yours. So then, what's all the hubbub, bub?

Actually, there's a lot more to learn, and fortunately, no lack of teachers. Estherham* is among the cream of the LOA crop. We humans are complicated emotional creatures filled with conflicting thoughts, and it turns out that wanting and believing aren't always so straightforward. Which is why many people fail to get the goods—you know, like the ones who tape the fake million-dollar bill to the ceiling —and end up pronouncing the whole thing a scam. They have bypassed some crucial studies, and their Cliff Notes cramming failed to land them a good grade on the final exam. Look, no one said Earth School would be easy (unlike Earth Girls). We can be as dense as the rest of our time-space reality. LOA truly is a law in effect 'round the clock, but becoming conscious of our participation in it is not a skill most of us have cultivated. However, we can get re-educated for the new age—like retraining for the new economy. Whatever that is.

---

* "Abraham," as the story goes, is an arbitrary name for the group of evolved non-physical souls speaking through and in conjunction with Esther Hicks. "Estherham" is probably the most apt term since it's a blending of personalities/entities, but I like to mix it up with "Abe" and "the Abrahams."

186

Not everyone gets bogged down in emotional complexities. I've seen inspiring prodigies who suddenly tuned in to this LOA stuff and quickly turned their lives around, as if someone had tapped them on the shoulder and told them their shoes were untied; 'twas a done deal. For the rest of us though, it takes some perseverance.

When I first learned about LOA back in the 1980s, it seemed to be all about writing affirmations. The thing is, affirmations are just words, and you've got to actually *feel* a thing to make it happen. You can't fake a vibration—the universe *knows*, man. But here's the important thing that's often glossed over: you can't *force* it either. If you're feeling desperate and hopeless, you can't make a quantum emotional shift to believing just by scribbling something on a piece of paper. You can't just jump across the canyon like Evel Knievel; you've got to take the emotional footbridge, step by step, however long it takes, and just decide to be okay with every interim footing you find yourself on.

As for the jargon, "the vortex" is a construct for a place or state of being in which everything you desire already exists in a vibrational format. To have it convert or transmute into the physical world, you've got to be a vibrational match to it. The solution to everything is essentially to "get in the vortex and then…" In other words, get happy. Bliss out before you visualize what you want or before you make an important decision, and solutions will effortlessly reveal themselves. Co-operative components (people, stuff, circumstances, timing) will be at your service, without any laborious striving involved. Abe points out that everything we desire is for one reason only: we think we'll feel better when we get it. Ironically, or maybe annoyingly so, we've got to feel better *first* so the things we want can show up and feel at home. The key to happiness, it turns out, is *being happy*. Brilliant.

Estherham's major contribution has been in explaining the value and use of our human emotional guidance system (EGS). Micro-managing *thoughts* is an impossible task, but *emotions* are there to give us easy-to-read signals about those thoughts. Feeling good is a green light, indicating alignment with your higher self, your purest intentions. Feeling crappy means the thoughts you've been thinking are not in your best interest. (It sounds inane until you try applying it on a continuous everyday basis.) It's empowering stuff, and a boon to anyone who's ever been criticized for being overly emotional. It's no wonder so many women gravitate to Abe-Hicks seminars. (What, you mean there's actually a *purpose* for those pesky emotions?) For some people, especially straight guys, it takes a little excavation work and dedication to make the emotional connection, as they've been taught to stuff it all down by societal mores born of the same arrogance that pronounces entire bodily organs or brain mass "useless" when the functions are not immediately obvious.

Beyond that scholarly achievement, those Abrahams are just dang funny. One of my favorite one-liners came after someone said "it's good to see you, Abraham." They replied, "it's good to be seen — normally we are just a nebulous mist." Their comedy and empowerment tour has created a cohesive community that amounts to nothing short of a tribal lovefest. What more do people long for?

In the workshops, people would get up in the "hotseat" for personal coaching, airing their psychological dirty laundry in the process. Estherham skillfully stepped each one through a customized emotional journey that was clearly transformational. I loved observing the changes in a person's face as they absorbed the insights. Most anyone listening derived personal benefit too, because we all have roughly the same challenges, and the answers are often far-reaching. It all comes down to cleaning up your vibration and claiming your sovereignty. But it's not for the weak. Taking full responsibility for what goes on in your mind can be daunting, and people are quick to relinquish their power, pointing to old patterns, childhood programming, societal beliefs, other people's needs and opinions. But Abe swoops in with the tough love, waking you from your victimhood slumber and reminding you that the power is right here, right now, in your very next thought. You can choose better-feeling thoughts once you become aware of your feelings. And beliefs are merely thoughts you think repeatedly, so you have control over those too. "You're making a big hairy deal out of all of this!" they were fond of saying, followed by uproarious laughter from the crowd. Sometimes I just need a wise-cracking ghost to remind me of such things. Or an incarnate wise man like Wayne Dyer does the trick too. But I needed to hear it approximately ten million times before it really sunk in.

Because there is no Law of Repulsion, whether we enthusiastically and frequently say "yes!" or "no!" to something, the universe brings us more of it. Whatever we give our energy to... *gets more energy*. And the stronger the emotional charge accompanying the thought, the more potent the boomerang experience. Therefore, criticism has got to go. All of it. Criticism of other people and things, but first and foremost of the self. Feeling good is the number one goal here. Change the channel to something you *do* like and "follow your bliss," as Joseph Campbell so righteously entreated us. Again, it's conceptually simple, but when you're stuck in the muck, it can be hard to pull yourself up by the proverbial bootstraps—and to extract or reclaim your individual thought-terrain from the collective neurotic mind.

To this end, Estherham advocates not giving a rip what other people think *and* not requiring anyone else to change in order for you to feel better. This is revolutionary, post-codependent stuff, and possibly the best interpersonal counsel I've ever heard. In other words, it's not my job to make others feel good because that's *their* job. "Everyone and everything is selfishly oriented," says Abe. I liked their system a lot.

So, yeah, they're bringing selfish back. But it's a bold new connotation because taking care of the self benefits everyone, whereas martyrdom causes problems. Selfish doesn't have to mean self-absorbed, unaware or unscrupulous—like the dopey kid in the front seat of a crowded city bus who stares, earbuds a-blaring, glued to his seat, as elderly persons and very-pregnant women teeter nearby, grasping handrails. Or the driver who pulls out and blocks a lane of traffic because she doesn't want to wait her turn for the right-of-way (I understand this is standard procedure in certain parts of Massachusetts). Prioritizing self-satisfaction wouldn't necessitate life becoming one episode of *The Young and the Clueless* after another. Hell, it already does resemble that more often than not, so what have we got to lose?

Following Abe's advice en masse would put an end to burnt-toast syndrome as a communicable disease. I can imagine a sort of well-oiled anarchy in which individuals are guided to do whatever pleases them at any given time, and everything works out synchronistically for all parties involved. Everyone would mind their own vibration! We'd stop seeing sociopathic behavior if everyone truly loved themselves: the would-be sociopath, in following his emotional guidance system, would realize how good it feels to be loving and thoughtful toward others. Okay, so call me an idealistic fool. Or an inspired visionary. Take your pick, because it doesn't matter what you think of me, see?

Not that I need for any of this vision to materialize, but I just like to put philosophies through the "universalization" test. I should point out that, with all that I've been saying here, there is an implication of being separate from other people, which is how we generally experience life. Yet I know this is an illusion; we are all part of the same invisible uber-rhizome like so many irises enmeshed at the earth's surface. That is the great paradox, is it not? We can adopt whichever viewpoint works at any given time. There really aren't any rules or laws... other than the Law of Attraction, of course.

And speaking of LOA, one way I like to think about this manifesting business is the act of leaning more heavily on the *yin* principle—allowing and drawing good things to me with minimal effort—versus the overt *yang* energy of going out there and making things happen, caveman style. Really it's about letting the yin goddess do her thing first, so as to wisely inform and inspire the yang work. In other words, loosening the reins from the grip of the conscious mind. Things can be so much easier than we've been led to believe. It's okay to kick back and trust more. And question the programming we've inherited from certain foaming-at-the-mouth ancestral religious folk, because many of us were ingrained with the imperative of working our butts off to earn every morsel—or worse, that we're "bad" if we don't. Hogwash.

Obviously the Abe-Hicks material is about so much more than, say, manifesting a car, even though that's what most people take away from *The Secret*. Estherham addressed, in a very satisfying way, my most pervasive existential question: "why am I here?" I'm here for the sheer joy of experience, thereby adding to the expansion of *all-that-is* consciousness. I haven't come to suffer, to repay old karma, to learn hard lessons. Maybe there's learning on the agenda, but school doesn't have to be a big drag. *Life is supposed to be fun.*

Life honestly did get a lot funner and easier when I started taking full responsibility for myself and for the only thing I truly have dominion over—my own thoughts—while letting the rest of the world off the hook. Getting into the habit of appreciating, even the tiniest of things, really helps with the vibration-raising. It's a decidedly different worldview from your average man on the street's *all-that-sucks* perspective. And it's not some project to be completed and checked off a list—it's an ongoing ethic from which I decided to operate. As Estherham says "you can't get it wrong because you never get it done." There will always be homework, as new situations arise that test my resolve, but it gets easier and more natural all the time. There will always be contrast or duality—identifying what I want through experiencing what I don't want—but the Abrahams helped me to comprehend the crucial role that pcontrast plays in our time-space continuum, rather than cursing it like I used to do.

Just because it's fun, here's an Abraham quote-cloud to help further elucidate their philosophy:

be true to your weird self * well-being truly does abound * you are an extension of non-physical source energy * abundance in all things is available to you * the joy is in the journey * you are so free that you are free to choose bondage * you are on the leading edge of thought * what you think and what you feel and what you experience are always a match, no exceptions * you are worthy beings * the thoughts you think determine the life you live * you are the vibrational writers of the script of your life and everyone else is playing the part you assigned to them * you are all perfect and expanding * source energy is always responding to your requests * start taking pleasure from your inner reality * look around less, imagine more * you do not need anyone else to align with your desire * be easy about it * there is not something you're supposed to do * if you want it and you relax, it will happen * there is great love here for you!

⸸ ⸸ ⸸

It all went down so easy, like a chocolate milkshake on a summer afternoon. I had already been thinking along these lines, but I'd never been this resolute. I'd been prone to second-guessing myself and allowing other people to make me feel wrong for this or that—or so I thought. Not so, anymore. It was me, and me alone, who had done the allowing of thoughts that led to negative feelings. Abe's advice was by far the most deeply empowering woo-talk I'd encountered. I was essentially giving myself license to unapologetically be me in all my imperfection, to prioritize my own needs, and simply be happy no matter what. I gladly jumped on board —literally.

Just a few weeks after that first workshop, I set sail on the Vortex of Attraction Cruise to the Panama Canal. Emboldened by a renewed sense of power and immortality, I threw financial caution to the wind, rationalizing the expenditure in several ways: soon I'd be settling down and getting back to a "normal" life once I moved to California, and it would be much harder to get away and take a cruise then, so I might as well do it now. Also, I reminded myself that I could easily kick off the planet at any time, so I should have a good time in the Now, and isn't that what money is for? I'd never been on a cruise ship but was intrigued with the idea (though admittedly, leery of the possibility of being outnumbered by cranky, demanding aging Americans). In younger days I would have shunned such a frivolous vacation, pronouncing it very Bourgeois and non-ecologically-correct. Ah, youth *is* wasted on the young. (It seems my twenties were largely focused on railing against things. My thirties turned to positive personal expression, while shedding the unnecessaries along the way, and now, in my forties, I was becoming completely free of remaining encumbrances and limitations. At least that's the plan.)

I loved being on that boat! The motion of the waves, the extensive culinary delights, the formal dress-up nights, the cheesy musicals, the swimming pools and hot tubs on deck, the dancing, the karaoke, the shore excursions… and of course, nostalgic thoughts of *The Love Boat*. Actually, there was a sweet couple who got married during one of our island stopovers; they had met on another Abraham cruise the year before. And new romantic partnerships were forming right before my eyes. (Hmmm, maybe the Vortex of Attraction is a dating game after all...) Well it goes to show that it wasn't all hens in this woo-flock. *

If life is supposed to be fun, a tropical cruise was certainly a good way to prove it. I went snorkeling in an outrageously turquoise warm-as-bathwater coral reef paradise. That was the day I conquered my snorkel-phobia. At last I understood that I simply could not breathe through my nose, no matter what, and that I needed to deliberately breathe only through my mouth. Duh. How is it that I never grasped that before? When you're "in the vortex" everything is easy, even things that used to be hard. It was a microcosmic expression of this brand new way of living: chill out, get a grip on emotional reality, develop positive expectations, and everything works out. I stopped hyperventilating and relaxed, and my entire body coursed with laughter as schools of bright blue-and-yellow-striped fish swam right underneath me, while undulating purple coral waved "hello!" from ten feet down. I was floating in a giant aquarium—an interloping, though not unwelcome, human addition to the edgeless tank. For the first time in months, I experienced pure unadulterated bliss and complete sensory immersion. And that was just day two of ten.

The days seemed to last forever—in a good way. We'd play, eat, learn, and play some more. I felt like I'd found my long lost family. Those Abrahamsters sure knew how to have a good time. But they also understood the importance of being responsible for their own feelings, even if they hadn't quite mastered the art. We're all works in progress anyway. They tended to be very open and easy to be with and I loved how it seemed like we'd always known each other (maybe we had?). We dove right in to the good stuff, dispensing with the usual formalities. No one even asked me what I *do*. I was tickled pink.

---

* Interestingly, while the workshops seemed to consistently bring in about thirty percent men, the hotseat was disproportionately populated by dudes— roughly seventy percent of the time. I have my own theories about this, but I'll just leave it for you to ponder.

At least those were the people I gravitated to. Like any crowd, it was a mixed bag. As you can probably imagine, the Abe way of thinking draws more than its share of narcissistic types. It makes perfect sense, because if I were a hardcore narcissist their advice would be music to my ears. Really, it's a fine line between selfish orientation and outright narcissism. There were also repeat attenders who had been coming to workshops for years but never seemed to actually implement Abe's guidance—perhaps adopting it as a purely intellectual pursuit? They were noticeably less fun, so I naturally avoided them.

A small subset of those intellectualizers became the self-deputized LOA police, ready to issue a summons for your every digression. Of course they mean well, but as my mother always said, the road to hell is paved with good intentions. It's a typical progression —when one first dives into this law of attraction stuff and gets enthralled with the potential of this "new" truth—to become hyper-vigilant, but proselytizing more often leads to resentment than happiness. Even so, panning out to the bigger picture revealed the importance of the LOA police in the crowd: it helped me implement the principles by cultivating imperviousness to other people's drama. And it helped me to get clear about how I don't—and therefore how I do—want to conduct myself. That ever-helpful mirroring thing, combined with the beauty of contrast. (Then again, I'm just narcissistically framing the issue in terms of my own needs here.)

Navigating through the Panama canal was fascinating (the huge ship we were on barely fit, with a mere two feet to spare on either side), and the experience lent itself nicely to a new Estherham analogy in our on-board seminars: our emotions are like the water in the locks. We can't make the eighty-foot vertical transition from one ocean to the other in one fell swoop, so we do it in stages. For instance, anger is a level up from depression or powerlessness. Or, from doubt you need to go through hope before you can get to belief and eventually to knowing.

This and so much more I learned on my seafaring vacation. I loved it so much that I booked another Abe cruise six months later— this time to Alaska. In between, I listened to hundreds of workshop recordings, in a pointed and joyful act of positive self-brainwashing. I became a full-fledged Abrahamster for a little while, as it felt incredibly good. My social world exploded in the best possible way. I'd found the community I had for years been seeking, only... it wasn't a traditional geographically-based community because many of my new friends were scattered around the globe. All those years I had been fixated on the hippie land commune idea I never imagined a cyber-community could bring me the same feeling of cohesive belonging. Of course I still love hanging out with friends in person, but since I love to travel, it's not a huge impediment. And if we're morphing into a telepathic society (it's fun to think so), then physical location will become less and less relevant. Until then, gah-bless the Interweb.

⚡ ⚡ ⚡

All teachers, even the best ones, have their limitations. When I was a young'n, someone once told me that "everyone has a piece of the truth." It took me a few decades to understand that, but now that I do, I'll offer this corollary: "...and no one has the entire Truth."

There was a tendency for certain devotees—not the majority by any means but a notable few—to deify Abraham and resist or even be threatened by critical thinking. Estherham's delivery had a faux-cockiness to it that was usually pretty humorous, but I suspected some of the followers were taking it very seriously. "We're brilliant," Abe was fond of saying, and people often referred to them as "infinite intelligence." I suppose that's just typical human stuff though—the desire for a guru, and the tendency toward misguided absolution. Maybe it's the biblical sounding name that inspires them?

Personally, I do not conceive of the Abrahams (or anyone else) being omniscient. If that were the case, they've been holding back on us. And that would be patronizing, which of course doesn't feel good, so I'm actually following their very advice in thusly scrutinizing them. Sure, Abe is super smart, with a broader scope than most of us, but *omniscient*? Hell no. Besides, it's a blend of entities speaking, and it's not hard to discern Esther's very human contribution to the mix at times, such as in the following snippet:

195

"Reduce your workload by 30% and increase your fun load by 30% and you will increase your revenues by 100%. And you will increase your productivity by 10,000%. (If there could be such a percentage.) More fun, less struggle—more results on all fronts."

Yes, there could be such a percentage. A god-like being would know that of course, but a sweet fun-loving grandmother might not.

On a few occasions, I could have sworn they were doling out conflicting or downright misleading information—for example, in explaining that our dreams are downloaded to us in the instant right before we wake up. Of course, it's widely believed that we dream throughout the night, especially during REM periods after a few sleep cycles. I'm no proponent of consensus thinking, but for me, firsthand experience and some fascinating research* reinforce the popular angle on dreaming. Granted, it is true that the answers Abe provides in the workshops are subject to misinterpretation when taken out of context, because they were talking to a specific person at a specific time about a particular situation. And I'd imagine that hotseat inquisitors receive an energetic response that is non-verbal and not necessarily obvious to observers. Ultimately, we each get what we need. It just underlines the value of critical independent thought.

When it came to esoteric subject matter such as alternate modes of consciousness, other dimensions—big-thinking cosmological stuff—I found Abe's assertions rather unsatisfying. Some things just weren't on the syllabus, despite their insistence that "nothing is off limits." It was sort of like going to biology class and asking questions about art history, then having the professor give you some authoritative-sounding response. Often that answer was given teasingly and in a slightly condescending tone, looping back to the basic notion that reality is what you make it, so if you think there are 47 dimensions, then there are. Fair enough, Abrahams. I wasn't ever seeking a one-stop-woowoo-shopping center, so I didn't mind the limitations.

---

* Renowned lucid dreaming researcher Stephen LaBerge conducted experiments in which there was real-time direct communication between the dreamer *while in the dreamstate* and the monitoring technician in the lab.

At one point I attended a local Law of Attraction weekly event where we would listen to Abraham seminar recordings and discuss them afterward. For a while, I was very happy to have this group in my life because it gave me some semblance of local community on my new home turf. The content was pretty compelling until the facilitator introduced a "live channel" who was obviously mimicking Esther Hicks—even adopting her peculiar mannerisms to a tee! But this woman's energy level was nowhere near that of Estherham's. She talked a lot about *joy*, but in such a blasé tone that made it wholly unpersuasive, if not downright ludicrous. They seemed like little kids playing grown-up games (they even set up a little hotseat and microphone), with the meeting facilitator wanting to be the Jerry Hicks of the show. I was far more entertained by some actual children I'd seen earlier that day in Starbucks pretending to order lattes and cappuccinos.

⚡ ⚡ ⚡

And so, it was the end of another mini-era. It hadn't been the Holy Grail it once seemed, but a major milestone just the same—a hugely instrumental stop on my emotional journey. It became time to fly out of the nest. I still like to take an Abe/LOA refresher course once in a while, but for the most part, the message has been indelibly etched into my brain and now permeates my way of living.

I've got more exploring to do outside Abe's realm of expertise, and probably I'll always find things to be curious about. They delivered a potent reminder to relax and enjoy the ride, and for that I'm very appreciative. I decided that being a straight-up pragmatical gnostic is too rigid, because there are so many intangibles to believe in these days. But there can be a sort of Nouveau Gnosticism, hinted at in this Estherham quote, that suits me just fine:

"The only way that you can ever know if something is of value to you is by the way it feels as you are receiving it."

Emotional GPS, lead the way. Onward… to further amusement.

16

CALIFORNOGRAPHY: DES VIGNETTES

"The mystery man came over
and he said: 'I'm outta sight!'
He said, for a nominal service charge,
I could reach nervonna t'nite…"
♫ Frank Zappa

A new friend of mine who I simply adored invited me to join her for a Kirtan chanting event at a local meditation center, so I jumped at the chance to check the place out while spending some quality time with her. We arrived early to avoid parking lot mayhem and leisurely stroll around the grounds. It was a sweet spot steeped in lush greenery with modest mountains standing by. The event hall itself was a pleasing piece of architecture, newly built with a huge vaulted tongue-in-groove wood ceiling and walls that seemed to consist only of glass for the purpose of showcasing the views. Fancy and/or schmancy to be sure. Maybe this was why we paid twenty-five bucks to get in.

The kirtankars, or stars of the show, were already onstage, sitting in lotus position before lit candles, engaging in banter about the success of their recent recording. One was a young woman in her twenties sporting hipster glasses and draped in Indian clothing; the other was a silver-haired man who'd probably spent more decades in ashrams than she'd been out of the womb. The usual white folks with adoptive Hindi names. Rahjneesh or something? (No, wait, that's a whole different can of worms.) The resident sound-couple who worked the mixing board was visiting with them and ostensibly stroking their professional egos—that is, if they were to have egos, which of course they did not. The background track playing sounded very much like the amplified hum of a fluorescent bulb.

Other attendees slowly filed in—some of them regulars with their own special pillows. One dude, in making an exuberant beeline to his mat, sideswiped a more slowly moving woman and failed to notice her perturbation. Eventually, a rather sad-looking man commandeered the microphone and in a monotone, almost robotic voice introduced the stars. "It's going to be a lot of fun" issued unconvincingly from his near-motionless lips. He turned the mic over to a tanned toned blonde woman who ended up playing the ringmaster role and doubling as a back-up singer. The fourth and final star was a guy playing a hand drum and sporting a suspicious little mustache. As introductory remarks were made signaling the start of the show, I noticed him buttoning his shirt up a little higher. Wise move I daresay; no need to distract the womenfolk from their spiritual questing. Blondie started talking about enlightenment and told us it's "no problem" if we don't get there tonight. What a relief. She asked how many people had attended one of their silent retreats and the woman next to me nearly clocked me in the head in her fervid attempt to let it be known that she was one of the serious devoted ones.

The music began. The two main singing stars had fantastic voices: very different styles that somehow meshed together. His was classic for this genre—it sounded exactly like you'd think this chanting stuff should sound. Close your eyes, and it's an Indian man before you singing. Hers was a voice that sounded classically trained but stylized in that modern R&B pop sort of way that comes from growing up watching American Idol on TV. For all I know, she might have been the one who sang that sappy ballad from The Little Mermaid. Interesting, superimposing a modern vocal style on this ancient stuff. (Therein lies the original spark of creation!) Mr. Star quickly taught the song to the audience so we could join in—an easy task because there were only two words. He laughingly admitted to knowing only about ten more from the Sanskrit language.*

While the four of them were onstage singing and playing various percussion instruments, the main accompaniment was prerecorded. Apparently a harmonium is typically used for kirtans. I don't know if that's what this was, but it totally sounded like a third grader practicing on the melodica he recently acquired from the Sears catalog. So when the chanting started in, it was a big relief to my ears. Sure, it gets a little boring with just two words, but that's the whole point of a kirtan, which means "to repeat"—it's call and response. Easy for people to partake of, not unlike square dancing. The participants, if they're lucky and willing, can join in, get whipped up into a frenzy and whisked away to Enlightenmentville.

In between musical numbers, MC Blondie narrated guided meditations with gag-me phrases like "notice your heart smiling at your belly," and gave us spiritual pep talks with quotations from long-ago-dead guys like Rama Krishna, expounding the merits of divinity

---

* I couldn't help but think of that hilarious Flight of the Conchords video where the guys pretend to know French in order to bag the chicks, then get exposed in the end for their fraudulence. At least this guy was upfront. Then again, that kind of vulnerable confessional could easily be just another ploy.

through selfless love. Selfless love… hmmm. Now there's a big ol' red flag. I don't know about you, but most of the trouble in my life has been caused by selfless love. I think it would be more accurate to call it self-sabotage.

"Keep coming back to the moment with uninterrupted remembrance," she petitioned. Then something about the "primordial awareness" and the bhakti path of devotion. Uh-huh. More about love… universal love, divine love, brotherly love, intimate love. Seems that every kind of love was kosher as long as it's not the dreaded *self-love*. Wow, are people still buying into that "self bad, martyrdom good" thing? It seems so passé. But, to each his own. The whole shenanigan was really just a show, all of us playing character roles—not unlike going to a Renaissance Faire or one of those famous battle reenactment thingies. Or maybe it was closer to a high school production of Jesus Christ Superstar. Whatever floats your boat, I say.

Speaking of boats, the dude a few rows ahead of me was wearing a Grateful Dead tie-dye that screamed "Ship of Fools" across the back. A woman near him sported an exquisite head of dreads adorned with silver and turquoise rings. Next to her sat one of those angelic faerie hippie mamas with her man and their spawn. It was mostly a caucasian crowd, more women than men, and roughly forty to sixty in age. Lots of shawls and flowy skirts and yes, of course, Indian garb. You gotta dress the part. Like wearing the pirate wench get-up to Ren Faire. (I didn't smell any patchouli though, in case you were curious.)

With the canned musical track up and running, the singing stars started out modestly and built up momentum, stirring up energy in the room. The drummer man became more and more enlivened until it looked like he was having convulsions from the neck up—all the while, miraculously, expertly keeping the beat. The young chick-singer smiled and shook her head rapturously, which, for some reason, kind of gave me the creeps. The music continued to crescendo and soon the first sputnik was loosed from the front row! Oh, he was feelin' it, alright. He could hardly contain himself. He got up and did that prayer-hands-to-the-face thing to the rest of us and then skipped off to the back of the room, exploding into noodle-dancing ecstasy.

Who's next? Oh, oh, looks like we've got a mat wiggler in row two. Then the clapping started in earnest.

The frenzy came to a boil, then simmered back down, giving way to the awkward non-silence of one hundred humans in a room together. Blondie guided us in meditation once again and asked "what does joy and delight *feel* like?" This struck me as an asinine question. I wasn't the only one balking at her schtick. I could feel a lot of people becoming restless. When she instructed us to keep our eyes closed, mine of course immediately popped open (always on cult-alert, or else garden-variety rebelliousness—take your pick) and I could tell the singing stars were not havin' what she was dishin' out. I could almost see their eyes rolling from where I sat. Clearly, she was cutting into their air time and changing the vibe not to their liking. To my delight, the sound of bullfrogs erupted outside, and this, coupled with the pastorally pleasing sight of deer grazing, was far more meditative than my inner landscape at the moment.

Blondie continued. "What are you sensing with your body right now?" Well, my nose couldn't help but sense that some bastard's been passing gas for the last half an hour. Whatever happened to selfless love? I mean, if you truly loved everyone else and not yourself, shouldn't you hold it in, no matter what, regardless of imminent gastrointestinal demise? Clearly *someone* had not been paying attention. I wished that Blondie would clam up and let the frogs take over the sermon.

Finally the meditation segment ended and it was time for another two-word extended dance jam, this one even less catchy than the first tune. The frenzy was reached more quickly this time, which I suppose could be attributed to a learning curve... or something analogous to what I call "white boy syndrome" whereby dancing occurs after a certain requisite amount of alcohol ingestion. The drummer's eyes bulged wildly while scanning the room. Most people were chanting along happily. One woman on the sidelines was jumping up and down like a pogo stick and waving her arms haphazardly while smiling broadly, imploring us with her eyes to follow suit (which I'm sure would have necessitated an ambulance, had we all complied at once). Then the dervish-fest started to deflate again, and my friend and I decided to split rather than subject ourselves to another round of Blondie's uninspiring treatises.

I asked my friend what she personally got out of the event. She said she simply enjoyed the sing-a-longs, but the meditation was a bit of a buzzkill. Not that either of us was a stranger to meditation, but you know, there's meditation and there's *meditation*. Thirty-one flavors to choose from and everybody likes different things at different times, right? I'm no joiner, so I'll probably never wholeheartedly participate in that kind of group chanting thing, especially in a language I do not understand. It just feels creepy and cultish to me. But honestly, I'm not disdainful of anyone else's participation. I just find it amusing, is all—a show to attend, another episode in the continuing saga of Eastern religion meets California. A sort of rapture-infused karaoke spectacle, with top notch singers performing inane repetitive twenty-minute cover songs. But for twenty five bucks they could have at least hired a *live* third grader to play the melodica. That's all I'm sayin'.

⚡ ⚡ ⚡

I was in Los Angeles over a long weekend for swing dance camp so I seized the opportunity to check out the Agape International Spiritual Center. One of my Abrahamster friends picked me up in her pimpin' automobile early Sunday morning, and soon we were standing in the first-time visitors' line waiting for the early-bird session to wind down. A super-funky version of the otherwise tired-and-true "Happy Birthday" was emanating out of the church. Presumably this was something they sang every time to anyone in the community celebrating a birthday that week. To our right was a much longer line of regulars eager to secure good seats. Certain people, including celebrities, had front row seats specially reserved for them; these were presumably the top tithers. With this one-time privilege, we were able to jet in when the doors opened and grab some prime real estate.

Inside, I was surprised to find the building in a very humble, less-than-pristine condition. We sat in the sort of '80s mauve armless chairs you'd find in an aging convention center, and the restrooms could've used a serious remodeling. Well, they were certainly not guilty of squandering funds on gilded architecture. The place was homey and plenty comfortable though, and we settled into our seats just in time for the opening meditation. It was an enjoyable one, minimally narrated with tastefully timed live piano accompaniment.

After a few minutes the members of the choir filed in, up, around, and behind the gorgeous grand piano on stage. These singers were clothed in an incredible array of bright colors and sparkles that combined to form a wiggly wonder wall. I marveled at the way two or three of them alone can strike the eye as garish, while the larger group synergy transformed them into a visual-symphonic masterpiece. It was symbolic eye candy, and unmistakably African in aesthetic. Up further still behind the choir, some of those clear plastic wavy roofing sheets had been cleverly hung as a backdrop, reflecting nicely the indirect and softly colored lighting. There were several dozen singers but, wisely, microphones were only given to Black folks for solos.*

I'd never been to a big box church before, so the large video screens seemed kind of wild. They were used to display read-along affirmations, quotes, advertisements for church programs, and occasionally, flashes of the whole scene from the perspective of the home-viewers watching via satellite broadcast. A few different Agape Practitioners took the podium to deliver inspiration and practical announcements—essentially, Reverend Michael Bernard Beckwith's warm-up acts. They included his incredibly energetic and youthful barefoot wife, Rickie Byars Beckwith, known affectionately as Rickie B.B. She played the piano and sang beautifully. There was much promotional fanfare about her new CD and book release, and toward the end of the program they played a musical video montage of her songwork that was pretty much an infomercial. I cringed slightly, thinking that maybe modern R&B gospel was not my favorite flavor of recorded music. But I loved the singing at Agape, and the house musicianship was top shelf—these cats had some serious chops. Some things are just better live, methinks.

---

* That's a joke, so please don't get your panties all in a bunch. But they really did only have African American soloists that day, honest! And they were fabulous.

Rickie B.B. is positively adored by the congregation (and why wouldn't she be?) In fact, the whole institution was nothin' but a big ol' LoveFest. As newcomers, we were pinned with purple ribbons and asked to stand up and bask in the love, which we did, willingly, gratefully. The regulars handed us each a card printed with a heart and a heartfelt greeting. I could feel the love oozing out all over the room, for reals. My mind flashed back to the time I'd stealthily attended a Black Baptist church years ago; I had been powerfully drawn in by the incredible music pulsing out through walls and windows. The preaching and proselytizing was hardcore, but I had successfully remained seated with poker face intact when they asked the newcomers to make themselves known. Agape was nothing like that; there were no untoward attempts at conversion or dogmatizing going on here.

Reverend Beckwith's sermon was most excellent: uplifting, real, non-condescending, inspired and inspiring. I've always liked the guy since I first saw him in *The Secret*. There's just something about him—a calm confidence, a presence that is so *likable*. His ego is not front and center, nor is it sublimated. Rather, it seems well-blended and balanced in his orientation to the world. He's quite funny at times and shows humility, saying things like "I'm just talkin' here… 'cuz I've got the mic!" Part way into his talk he became deeply rapturous, as a good preacher must, but he was peddling self-empowerment, unlike his traditional counterparts. The theme-of-the-month was "Dare to Live." He spoke of vibration and "set point" (i.e., point of attraction in Abe-speak) for our experiences, of seeking and accepting inner guidance, of turning away from the negative programming of the news, which is really the "olds" parading as the news. His candor surprised and impressed me. I would not have predicted the inclusion of a media critique in this man's spiel.

Of course there were sing-a-longs. Oh you betcha I was up on my feet a-clappin' and a-carryin' on just like all the others. Good times. At the close, they reprised the funky version of Happy Birthday, and it just happened to be the good Reverend's own birthday that day. He proceeded to do push-ups on stage while looking very fine in his fine brown suit—the kind of push-ups that are done with

206

only one foot on the floor. Damn, that man has got it goin' on. My friend told me the Internet had apparently been scrubbed of data because no one seems to know his real age. Surely he's older than he looks. Not that it matters. After the service, my friend and I got in a short meet-n-greet line and we got to hug the birthday boy. It was a sweet moment filled with warm fuzzy good juju, setting the tone for the rest of the day and the rest of my tenure in L.A.

I left with a packet of literature that included various color glossy productions, some with "meditative thoughts" , one explaining the Agape movement, a thick little booklet called "Inner Visions" (a nod to Stevie Wonder, no doubt), and naturally an envelope or two, should I be inclined to check-writing activities. The materials mostly had that same marketing look as the Jehovah's witness and Scientology junk mail that shows up in my mailbox, and this gave me pause for a moment, I must admit.

Another packet item entitled "Spiritual Principals [sic] of the Agape Movement" listed the following seven practices that "form the matrix of individual spiritual evolution":

- Meditation
- Affirmative Prayer (which I interpret as co-creating your own reality)
- Life Visioning (ditto—Manifesting, part two)
- Sacred Service (hmmm... this is a little fuzzy. I guess it *does* feel good to provide service but only when it's what you want to be doing, not following some arbitrary mandate)
- Spiritual Study (construable as simple truth-seeking)
- Spiritual Community (does Facebook count?)
- and lastly...

Tithing. Well, it *is* a church after all. A very funky, cool, new-thinking church, but a church nonetheless. I don't know, there's just something about that word that hearkens back to the old bogus pay-your-way-into-heaven schemes. Sure, Agape has bills to pay and they're providing a valuable service. It's not that I begrudge them any fundage, and I certainly can't disagree with the idea that abundance is intimately connected to generosity via two-way energetic cash flow, but... I guess I'm like a cat sometimes. It's gotta be *my* idea.

⚡ ⚡ ⚡

Like a certain cat who was so curious about candle flames that she seared her whiskers on a few occasions (not naming any names), I keep trying yoga periodically.

I'm not sure what came over me this time. I guess I'd been on an imperceptibly slow physical decline that became suddenly perceptible. It had been a while since I wielded hammers and saws on an everyday basis, so things had started to atrophy. But perhaps I was also unduly influenced by my new environment in California. I was surrounded by the so-called "beautiful people" and feeling uncharacteristically insecure. I think Marin County must have the highest per capita gym membership and hair dye consumption rates in the nation. Even the crazy woman at the bus stop is well-coiffed with a fresh mani-pedi.

It sometimes crosses into the realm of bizarre and surreal, this fixation on youthfulness and outward appearances. I was in line at the credit union one day, and the customer in front of me was presumably twenty-something from the looks of her attire, svelte body, and long blond wavy hair. I was becoming a tad impatient, because the teller was taking an inordinate amount of time explaining to this woman how debit cards worked. I was thinking "WTF, girl, have you been living under a rock or something?" When they were finally through, she turned around and I got the shocking eyeful of a seventy year old woman's face, almost like a shrunken head—over-wrinkled, probably from too much tanning. Maybe she lacked the funds, if not the motivation, for injections or surgery. One can only surmise.

Anyway, it seemed as if yoga was becoming a societal requirement, an inevitable part of life somehow—like going to church in small town Wyoming circa 1860. God knows my meatsuit certainly needed some stretching, if not a complete recombobulation. So I ambitiously signed up for a one-week trial membership at a local yoga studio (that was ambitious for me). I planned to attend daily, but after just one class, I dropped all pretense of returning.

Admittedly, I picked the worst possible day to begin. It was a crowded Sunday morning class—so crowded that people had to stagger themselves down the rows so that every other person stood on the back (or front) of their mats. Wall-to-wall humanity. It was an odd arrangement too, because the instructor was in the back. I arrived early and set up my mat near the far wall, thinking *I* was in the back. When class began in earnest, awakening me from my little meditation-nap, everyone was facing me, and that big ol' mirror on the wall let me know, just in case I had any doubt, that people were staring at me disapprovingly. Yikes.

Or maybe they were just cranky, this crowd of mostly women in fancy yoga-wear and strict countenances that let you know they are very serious about their "practice." The room was warm—really warm. It wasn't *that* kind of yoga but, rather, someone's idea of a hybrid model, allegedly designed for all skill levels. But the overpopulation of hot sweaty bodies raised the irritability factor significantly. I wanted to open a window but refrained, wary of impending condemnation. It was weird how I'd become this meek person all of a sudden.

They don't give out yoga mats at this place (can you blame them? ew, I wouldn't want to clean them), and I don't own one, so I'd brought along my old trusty exercise mat. It's a garish shade of blue, and the kind of mat that's thick and spongy, which my bones totally love. When I came in, the instructor sort of looked at it sideways and said, "well, it's not exactly *evil*, but..." He warned that it would become soaked with my own sweat before long. I thought, "no problem, that's why I have this towel to cover it." It was a cushy set-up but clearly so out of vogue as to garner looks of horrified scorn. That and my randomly cobbled "work-out" attire. The mirror seemed to amplify my fat rolls in the presence of those extreme hard-bodies. Not a pretty sight in bright lighting. It surprised me to find myself thinking these thoughts, as if an alien was taking over my brain again —not the same one from the Mike-insanity days, but perhaps a second cousin from another planet.

209

For some incalculable reason, the guy behind me moved his mat way up so it was adjacent to and nearly overlapping mine. He was the only one in his row who wasn't following the staggered pattern. Perhaps he thought he had a better plan and that the rest of us should follow him instead? There was nowhere for me to go. It was incredibly annoying but I just couldn't find the right words and timing to air my grievance, knowing that the entire room was privy to my subtlest move or utterance.

Some poses I could do well enough. Others were ridiculous for the current state of affairs in my body. At times I've been downright pissed off in yoga class—usually about the fifth round of downward dog followed by that thing where you're supposed to magically transport your feet from the back of the mat to the front in one fell swoop. If you happen to have a waist that is about two-thirds of the way up your body, this is damned near impossible. So I typically would stop and do a child's pose or something less taxing. I couldn't see the instructor anyway, so I had to improvise half the time. At least I was able to throw my fragile athletic-ego a few crumbs when we'd do those standing-on-one-leg poses because my balance was pretty good, despite the "evil" foam mat I was perched on. (Incidentally, the only sweat that landed on that thing was from Mr. "I'm parking my mat up your ass" Yogi Neighbor. Yick.)

Cartoonish as it was, the scene was all too familiar. Every time I tried yoga, about 15 minutes into the class I just wanted to get the hell out of there. I relished the corpse pose at the end. But why bother? I could do that at home. Well, maybe I was just in it for the entertainment value. This particular class, despite its annoying parts, was more amusing than most because the instructor had that classic gay man's inflection in his voice and was fond of calling out people's names in commendation. "Good job, Sheila!" "Go for it, Anne!" "That's right, Steve." "You got it Sandra!" It was pure Romper Room.

At one point, while attempting some ridiculous pretzel-like configuration, I had the very satisfying realization that it was all way, way, *way* too much work. Like the "efforting" or "action journey" that Estherham speaks of as being so unnecessary—the act of paddling upstream. Ah! Could I not use my mental-energetic powers to consciously reshape my physical form, to transform my cells and whatnot? Preposterous as that sounds, I thought it would be easier and far more delightful.* The mere thought of it caused me to lighten up — I think I even dropped a pound or two. No, wait, that was probably from sweating.

Of course, lots of people genuinely enjoy yoga. I can only ever speak for myself. This was just another area where I learned to apply the "Life is Supposed to be Fun" manifesto and made some further changes. When, upon closer investigation, something turns out to be a "should do" or an "ought to do" disguised as a "really want to do" then I'm calling bullshit on it. I'm fully embracing the Ben & Jerry's bumper sticker philosophy: "If it's not fun, why do it?" (mmmmm, ice cream...) Just for the record, I don't abhor *all* exercise. I'm just giving myself permission to openly admit that yoga is a four-letter word.

I also understand that a lot of people consider yoga their "spiritual practice." Well, the term kind of cracks me up because it seems to me that everything and everyone is derived from *spirit*, or source energy, so Jerry Springer and motocross are every bit as spiritual as a Buddhist temple. And since we're all inherently "spiritual" already, what is there to *practice*? I do know, however, that any time I'm able to get quiet and stem the incessant chatter of the monkey mind, good stuff flows more readily — like peacefulness, calmness, happiness, guidedness, groundedness, centeredness, inner knowing, alignment, love, joy, connectedness, yada yada. So if "power yoga" — or chanting with the Hari Krishnas, windsurfing, motocross, you name it — is the thing that helps you quiet *your* wild mind, then more power to you.

---

* Interestingly, a few weeks later I discovered the woman known as "The Donut Whisperer." This gal has specific expertise in applying Law of Attraction principles to diet and exercise (or *not* dieting and exercising, to be more accurate) and she's living proof of what's possible. It's a brilliant perspective, because she figured out that thoroughly enjoying your food without worry, guilt, fear or regret actually makes you eat less. Hedonism in the service of health — a win-win proposition. I still wanted to quantum jump into a new meatsuit, but I found her stuff pretty inspiring and right on.

211

So… I went to a phony psychic. I didn't really mean to. It's just that I was curious about those neon signs permanently affixed to certain San Francisco storefronts and I had this loose theory that if the psychic stayed in business in one spot long enough, then it must be legit. But no. Bad theory, no donut.

I went for the cheapest option on the menu — a twenty-minute reading. She ushered me into her space with what seemed like genuine human warmth at first, and asked me to choose from a small number of topics to focus on (*there's* a red flag). She had a deck of cards, but it wasn't a real tarot deck. They were more like the blunt kindergarten scissors equivalent of tarot — extra large, and less than half the normal number of them. She proceeded to place every last one of them down, swiftly and without hardly looking at them, building a chateau shape on the table of her makeshift altar. Her cards were extremely worn out. I wondered how long she had been carrying on like this, as she was probably thirty years old at the most.

Before she began the reading, she asked me in a rather serious tone if I wanted her to tell me everything she saw, even if it was negative. I told her, "sure, don't hold back, I can handle it."

She then stared deeply into my eyes and said very disparaging but generic things. It was almost laugh-out-laudable. The session was nearly over when the topic switched to her energy healing services. She had thoroughly discussed all that was wrong with me and now she was offering to fix it with a chakra balancing for only $99. Ummm… yeah. I politely declined. The idea of balancing chakras is sort of like finishing the laundry (or the mail — just ask a postal worker, it never ends) and she was probably about the last person on earth I would want messing with my energy circuits. Besides, I could do it myself (and so can you… if you think you can).

I thanked her and left her second story rented space, amazed and amused as I walked down the city street in the beautiful sunshine. I wasn't concerned about the thirty bucks I'd spent; it was a reasonable edutainment fee. But I puzzled over the economic sustainability of her operation. Were there actually repeat customers? I couldn't help but pity them for their gullibility. I wondered if there had been dramatic scenes taking place where the rare indignant customer publicly demands a refund and a "coming clean" on her part.

I was also stunned to realize that I hadn't really encountered a full-on charlatan until now. Though I'd sometimes doubted the information supplied to me during readings, this experience made it crystal clear as to who was and wasn't faking it. It gave me newfound appreciation for Patti and Lisa French and the other truly talented seers I'd known. Perhaps this pseudo-psychic chick had started out on an honest footing, but found herself unable to consistently deliver the goods on demand, so she fell into an unscrupulous routine? Then again, maybe I was giving her too much credit.

⚡ ⚡ ⚡

A few weeks later, my lovely friend Anita paid me a visit from Europe, so I took her on a scenic drive down the resplendent California coast. We stopped in at Natural Bridges State Park which, to my surprise, had partially lost its luster after the sea reclaimed much of the impressive bridge-shaped rock. (That didn't stop the state from charging full priced admission.) It was one of those poignant reminders that nothing—not even stone—is immune to change.

As we sat there eating lunch and gazing out on the dazzling blue Pacific Ocean, I spied a surfer inside the curl of a huge wave. Fully in the green room, dude! Wow, exciting. With my eyes I followed the wave to shore... only... quickly I realized something unusual was going on. When the wave broke, no one was there. The subsequent waves were much smaller and tamer than the one apparently I alone had just seen, and the real flesh-and-blood surfers were in a different area altogether. Had anyone actually been surfing in the place I was looking, they would have smashed into some pretty gnarly rocks. But maybe that was precisely what had happened, only at another point in time? If it was a ghost, I figured he was a smart one, because I'd heard stories of people who die and relive their last moments over and over again, and this one seemed to be reliving just

213

the glorious part of his final experience. At least that was the segment I perceived.

Though I'd never had a visual experience quite like that before, I have felt the presence of a discarnate person in this physical realm. When I bought my first house and got the keys, I rushed over that night and let myself in, too excited to wait until the next day. To my chagrin, a loud alarm sounded. I was embarrassed and concerned about disturbing my new neighbors, but relieved when the thing eventually timed out. The next day I called the real estate agent to inquire about disabling the thing and she was equally surprised. "What? There *is* no alarm system. The house has been vacant for a year and no one's paid the alarm company fee, so it can't possibly be active." Huh. I went back to my new home and spoke aloud to the previous owner who had died in the house, thanking her for protecting the joint and assuring her that it was now in good hands. It may have looked and sounded stupid, but I really *felt* something in there.

And now this "surfer-ghost" had cropped up out of nowhere, unsolicited. Clairvoyance was still a rare touch-and-go thing for me, so this was kind of a big deal. I don't really know what it is I saw in the ocean. Maybe it *was* an apparition. Then again, maybe it was a case of "bleedthrough" between different realities? What if I just happened to glance into an alternate holographic universe for a few seconds, perhaps a movie-like projection of someone's thoughts that I picked up on? Like some guy on his lunch hour day-dreaming about surfing — his thought creates a reality *somewhere...* a reality among infinite realities. The question then becomes: why did I tune in to that specific reality at that particular moment?

I don't know, but it was cool. The magic ingredient was that I had been very relaxed, not particularly focused either ocularly or mentally, and was not consciously trying to achieve anything other than eating a sandwich. It was a ripple of wonderful weirdness in my day, and I was not at all concerned about my mental health or whether anyone else would understand or believe me. (And Anita was cool with stuff like that.) I wanted more, rather than less, weirdness. Well, okay, maybe not while I'm driving. And nothing as crazy as Richard Bartlett's reality. But a little more of that supernormal perception on a regular basis would be just swell. I suppose if I just relax and stay open, that's exactly what I'll get, because if I've learned anything at all it's that when it comes to intentions, "set it and forget it" is where it's at.

17

IT'S THE END OF THE WORLD AS I KNEW IT AND I FEEL FINE

"I've never been so alone and I…
I've never been so alive."
♫ Third Eye Blind

In dreams there is often a distinct feeling of solitude. There may be other people around and a lot going on, but it still seems like a projection, a made-up adventure to navigate—a movie to watch while simultaneously playing the starring role. In a way, I've begun living my waking life in a more dream-like fashion with that strong sense of sovereignty: alone but not lonesome. It's just a useful overlay on the template of reality, because being truly alone is not even possible.

Life can seem like a video game at times. I walk down the street, enjoying whatever stimuli I encounter—including the thoughts in my own head, as I'm beginning to regard them as just another observable thing that happens. I smile at people and maybe they smile back (score!) or maybe they scowl (buzz!), but it doesn't matter—it's only a game. It's not that I've turned into a zombie. It's just that I've got this auto-generated fun-vibe streaming live in my mind most of the time, and I don't necessarily require playmates. I think I'm finally starting to grasp what the Buddhists have been saying all these millennia. Some of them are a bit too somber for my tastes, but I think I get their drift.

Speaking of somber, I read Eckhart Tolle's *A New Earth* at the same time I was diving into the Abraham-Hicks material, and found the two quite complementary and equally moving. In many ways, they were saying the same things in markedly different voices. Tolle is more stick and Abraham, more carrot (and more *schtick*). Either way, the message is essentially this: "hey, look, *you* are the one holding the carrot so why don't you just give it to yourself already?" Eckhart seems a wee bit judgmental in wanting you to choose certain carrots over others, whereas the Abrahams encourage you to go for the biggest, juiciest carrot-of-your-dreams. I suppose that's the difference between a human sage and a gang of never-incarnated benevolent hoodlums.

I figured something out. It's ridiculously simple, but to me it is profound. It's about the distinction between being judgmental versus being observant, descriptive, or just having and expressing personal preferences. It occurred to me that judgments are moral proclamations of things being good or bad—sweeping statements of right or wrong—saying essentially, "I do (or do not) approve of this, and there *should* be

218

more (or less) of it in the world." But preferences are simply likes and dislikes, which we all have, as sure as we've got these names, meatsuits and personalities. I can dislike something without railing against it; I simply prefer less of it showing up in my personal reality. So I ignore it to the best of my ability and focus on other stuff that I like better. It works. On the other hand if I really really like something, I don't need to push it on anyone because life will naturally bring me into rendez-vous situations with people who like the same stuff. I think it's essential to be okay with what you like or don't like, because otherwise you're just judging yourself. Which interferes with fun, so that's no good. (Oops, I just made a judgment. Dammit, Debbianne. Wait, now I'm judging myself. Dammit again!)

Anyway, by focusing on the *feeling* part of it all, I find it easy to cut to the chase. As far as I can tell, the only harm of judgmentalism lies in generating resistance within the self—that is, the wanting or needing for things to be different, the lack of acceptance of what is, as-is. But it's a personal thing, and words may fail us. Other people don't necessarily know how I *feel* and whether or not I'm generating resistance when I'm describing what I observe. Look, I may be laughing at your tin foil hat, but I'm not labeling you wrong or stupid or saying you shouldn't wear it, or that we should start a federal campaign to ban tin foil hats. My vibration is up, up, up, and I can choose to feel satisfied in my self-appointed and self-anointed role of Highly Amused Human (HAH).

Cyndi Lauper was right—girls *do* just wanna have fun. In a way, things have come full circle. The world I inched away from a few years ago seemed party-obsessed and felt hollow to me then. Now, I choose my compadres based on how much fun we have together. But it's a different flavor of fun, to be sure. In a sense, the bar has been raised. It's fun *plus* freedom—freedom from emotional embroilments.

Some old friendships have faded away. You might say, in woo-speak, that we're no longer in vibrational accord. It comes down to this: if all you have in common is nostalgia, and the Present experience isn't very fun, what's the point in persevering? Usually the motivation is guilt. But just like those leaflet pushers on the street, you don't have to accept what they're handing you. People are fond of saying that "life is too short" or "you only live once" but I say life is eternal and too potentially joy-filled to linger for long in Judgmentville. People in the habit of dropping J-bombs simply get de-prioritized in my life. I still think fondly of them, but I might not want to spend time with them. I give myself unabated permission to decide what types of energies and situations I want in my life, and there can be no guilt or obligation unless I willingly sign on to it (which I won't... anymore). The friendships that continue to survive and thrive through all the twists and turns are the ones with built-in breathing room: we offer each other love and acceptance, sans strings. That's the only way to fly.

I had a dream about a formerly close friend who's no longer in my waking life. In it, she and I were plotting to dress identically and outlandishly at a social gathering while making no acknowledgement that anything unusual was going on—as a gag to play on our other friends. That pretty much sums it up: from the soul's perspective, it's all just a game we set up and enact. Life *is* but a dream.

I'm pretty convinced that the twofold key to happiness is levity and letting everyone off the hook—including, and *especially*, me. Self-love is the bomb-diggity. That's what I apparently came here to master, and things are right on schedule. Everything and everyone is okay. We're all free. Life is beautiful. That's my reality and I'm stickin' to it.

⚡ ⚡ ⚡

Once upon a time, I was hell-bent on becoming clairvoyant. I've made some progress in that direction, though I don't usually get the crisp well-defined visuals I was seeking. And the information is hit-or-miss, rather than on-demand. Of course, it would still be super cool to see auras, but if I never get the magical Viewmaster of my dreams, well, I can live with that. The thing is, I realized that I'm already a first-class clairsentient. So I started focusing on honing the tool, improving the interpretation and reaction time, rather than trying to cultivate a new superpower. It was like an after-school special where the moral is to appreciate the gifts you have and not covet your neighbor's. I also get the clairaudient hook-up every once in a while—

you know, the old voices-in-the-head gag.   Or straight up claircognizance (direct down-loads of knowingness). Regardless of the para-mechanism employed, the more I trust, the more fruitful the information is, and in turn, the more warranted the trust.   It's a judicious cycle.

The hunger for information has largely been sated, as most of my pressing questions have either been addressed or reformulated as to no longer induce vexation.   And I've noticed that I only have a strong desire for outside guidance when I'm feeling insecure; otherwise I'm content to be my own guru. Not in a left-brained know-it-all way, but in trusting that *some* part of me always has the 411.   The dreamstate is usually a safe bet when my conscious mind is otherwise preoccupied.   Despite the fact that some things seem inherently unknowable (at least from this earthbound perspective), other basic truths continue to shake down and re-present themselves. I extract the useful constructs along the way without getting too attached to any of them, because they always seem to become stepping stones rather than resting places.

Anyway, intellectual knowing can be overrated. Just for fun, I recently went for a tarot card reading and the chick said some glowing things about my writing and told me I ought to get out into nature more often. Is she "right"? Does it matter, when it feels good? Call me delusional, but I'd much rather be happy than right if it comes down to that kind of division.

I still play with energy healing sometimes — out of necessity when something becomes imbalanced, or as an experiment with friends or strangers (for example, sending stealth grounding energy to a crying baby on an airplane. It does work... if you think it will). But the vocational impulse has pretty much vanished, just like all those other thought-bubbles that arose and popped during the Crisis days.   I suppose it's no longer a mystery to me, despite the fact that new modalities appear on the scene continuously. But more importantly, I mostly don't feel like there's anything to heal. I no longer consider certain foods better or worse than others, or worry about plastic packaging or microwaves or whatever the threat-of-the-month may be. I just go with what feels best in the moment. Mostly my habits haven't changed, but I've subtracted from the equation any anxiety that was present, and replaced it with appreciation. Move over fear—bliss mongering is the new order of the day.

Why not embrace *ignore-ance*? It's a vibrational universe, so turning away from the unwanted makes all the sense in the world to me. If I consistently get happy and full of ease, my overall vibration is inhospitable to dis-ease. It's like the ultrasound cleaning tool my dentist uses: the plaque has no chance of holding on—it gets vibrated right on outta there. If I should croak and they cut open my meatsuit and find all sorts of scary things that prove me wrong, so be it, because I'd rather have fun here and now than worry about that remote possibility. Worrying would be a supreme squandering of my energy.

↯ ↯ ↯

When I look back at all my shenanigans, I'm stunned at how skillfully orchestrated it's all been. For instance, when Mike and I were ready to buy land together, the project was foiled. We found a parcel that had languished on the market for two years, but the owners suddenly and inexplicably revoked the listing mere hours before our offer came in. What felt like frustration and disappointment at the time was clearly a godsave in retrospect. Unbeknownst to them, those property sellers were cooperative components to the maneuverings of my higher self—that invisible hand that rescues me when I veer off the road into a ditch—and I'm sure it served them personally, as well. We're all dancing in this elaborate show together.

There have been times when I received the marching orders and dutifully carried them out, even though I doubted the wisdom of such an act—selling my home, to cite a trivial example. It was almost as if I'd been overtaken, and wasn't really sure why I was doing what I was doing. In time, I saw how it was all necessary and desirable for the unfoldment, that The Management really is competent, and that my internal resistance to that guidance was the only real source of Crisis.

I jumped on the Abraham-Hicks bandwagon in what seemed like its heyday. And what a fun hayride it was. Impulsively, I signed up for the Alaska cruise on what turned out to be the last day of registration, and that one magical week at sea connected me to some of the most amazing, aware, beautiful, fun-loving people I know and love. The Abrahamster circuit was like spring and summer immersion school at the Church of Feel Good (boatloads more fun than Summer Vacation Bible School) and it was exactly what I needed for the finite time I was soaking in it. As a rule, I seemed to always meet the right person or pick up the ideal book at the perfect time and place. Sometimes the pretense for getting me there gave way underneath me once I was effectively lured, but I started getting used to that. It gets easier to release attachments when you stop forming them in the first place.

At any rate, I have to stand back and applaud the Masterminders for pulling it all off. I've even come to appreciate how a cyst came to *assist* me in re-aligning myself. The whole world's a mirror—albeit sometimes the fun-house variety—and the reflections are ingeniously helpful when you've got the gumption to look them in the eye.

As for my gypsy blood, there was a time I believed myself to be ungrounded or malcontented, unconsciously acting out unhealthy childhood patterns because my family had moved around so much when I was a kid. My new perspective is that it is a gift, this wanderlust, to be so open to new experiences. Familial patterning need not be a negative thing—that was just a belief, and a belief is merely a thought I'd gotten into the habit of thinking. Voila! it's gone. The reasons I chose my birth family are now plain to see. That challenging bio-brood made it possible for me to launch myself into the world and become strong and independent. For that, I am filled with appreciation. They've acted out their roles flawlessly.

Anymore, I hardly indulge in regret or backward pondering. It's just as easy to don the rosy spectacles, and it becomes as automatic as breathing after a while. Of course I still can get waylaid occasionally in some emotional conundrum, but there's a calmer saner voice in the background reminding me that "this, too, shall pass." Those trials come around less and less often, but when they do, my lag time to emotionally pivot has been on the steady decline. So I pat myself on the back for becoming quick at the switch. Sometimes a song snippet will come to the rescue in my head, like "it won't mean a thing in a hundred years…" I remind myself that I'm just having another human experience in a lifetime that might be equivalent to the blink of an eye, and that usually does the trick.

Maybe it's even my last spin around the Earth block? Astrologer Bill and a few others had suggested this was the case, and I rather liked the idea. I recall him advising me that the best thing I could do would be to gather around me a critical mass of "beloveds" who will happily see me off to the next phase ("Have a great trip! Bon voyage!") rather than hold me back. Now I have just that—a circle of friends who understand that death is merely a transition, and who install no tethers in my back.

That whole alien business (alien-pod scapegoat jokes notwithstanding)—about being from this planet or that star system— no longer puzzles me. After all my woo-training, I figure I'm simply derived from source energy or conscious stardust or what-have-you, just like everyone and everything else around here. The idea of having a specific location as an origin seems like a flawed premise—stemming from the grand illusion of linear time—that implies a beginning and an ending to things. Probably I've got tons of soul-cousins (or other parts of me? …you know, chips off the old soul-block) out there in other realities and that's what the legitimate psychics are picking up on when they say such things during a reading. At this point, I'm not particularly bothered by it nor curious about it. I'm mostly content to spend quality time with my soul-peeps here on Earth, and be in the Now. At least for now.

⚡ ⚡ ⚡

Whether or not it's my last sojourn here is one of those moot and unknowable factoids, but what I *do* know now is that I can willfully leave at any point, free from guilt or moral repercussion. A few years ago I was *eager* to leave, coming from a dark murky place where life felt like an albatross. But now my heart is light. I'm willing to stick around and see how much more joy I can squeeze out of this ride. Once I feel that I've seen, heard, felt, smelled, tasted, learned, shared and experienced enough in this realm, then I'll get excited about my next big adventure, whatever or wherever that may be. I like Franco DeNicola's analogy of alternate movie endings for a person's life—that set of infinite branching realities to choose from. What'll it be?

In the meantime, there are still things and experiences I'd like to manifest (an out-of-body experience would be sweet... or a juicy MANifestation), for to be alive is to constantly identify new aspirations. It's a natural part of the system—the master plan, the great expansion—and not something to be curtailed or pooh-poohed. I launch these rockets of desire, just as we all do. But I'm feeling no particular burning urgency or attachment to outcomes anymore. I occasionally observe myself slipping into the role of Roadblock, even rendering an Emmy-worthy performance for a minute, but I'm okay with that too.

Acceptance precedes change, and everything yields to change... eventually. Sometimes life feels like a holding pattern or even backward motion, but rest assured, the goods are always en route and when the timing is right, the truck dumps 'em right out in front of you on the road. And you may look at the stuff and exclaim that it's the wrong truckload, but time and hindsight reveal that the universe makes no mistakes with our orders.

Lightning Source UK Ltd.
Milton Keynes UK
UKOW050318260113

205403UK00001B/123/P